THE PALESTINIAN AUTHORITY'S INTERNATIONAL CRIMINAL COURT GAMBIT: A TRUE PARTNER FOR PEACE?

HEARING

BEFORE THE

SUBCOMMITTEE ON
THE MIDDLE EAST AND NORTH AFRICA

OF THE

COMMITTEE ON FOREIGN AFFAIRS
HOUSE OF REPRESENTATIVES

ONE HUNDRED FOURTEENTH CONGRESS

FIRST SESSION

FEBRUARY 4, 2015

Serial No. 114–3

Printed for the use of the Committee on Foreign Affairs

Available via the World Wide Web: http://www.foreignaffairs.house.gov/ or http://www.gpo.gov/fdsys/

U.S. GOVERNMENT PUBLISHING OFFICE

93–158PDF   WASHINGTON : 2015

For sale by the Superintendent of Documents, U.S. Government Publishing Office
Internet: bookstore.gpo.gov   Phone: toll free (866) 512–1800; DC area (202) 512–1800
Fax: (202) 512–2104   Mail: Stop IDCC, Washington, DC 20402–0001

COMMITTEE ON FOREIGN AFFAIRS

EDWARD R. ROYCE, California, *Chairman*

CHRISTOPHER H. SMITH, New Jersey
ILEANA ROS-LEHTINEN, Florida
DANA ROHRABACHER, California
STEVE CHABOT, Ohio
JOE WILSON, South Carolina
MICHAEL T. McCAUL, Texas
TED POE, Texas
MATT SALMON, Arizona
DARRELL E. ISSA, California
TOM MARINO, Pennsylvania
JEFF DUNCAN, South Carolina
MO BROOKS, Alabama
PAUL COOK, California
RANDY K. WEBER SR., Texas
SCOTT PERRY, Pennsylvania
RON DeSANTIS, Florida
MARK MEADOWS, North Carolina
TED S. YOHO, Florida
CURT CLAWSON, Florida
SCOTT DesJARLAIS, Tennessee
REID J. RIBBLE, Wisconsin
DAVID A. TROTT, Michigan
LEE M. ZELDIN, New York
TOM EMMER, Minnesota

ELIOT L. ENGEL, New York
BRAD SHERMAN, California
GREGORY W. MEEKS, New York
ALBIO SIRES, New Jersey
GERALD E. CONNOLLY, Virginia
THEODORE E. DEUTCH, Florida
BRIAN HIGGINS, New York
KAREN BASS, California
WILLIAM KEATING, Massachusetts
DAVID CICILLINE, Rhode Island
ALAN GRAYSON, Florida
AMI BERA, California
ALAN S. LOWENTHAL, California
GRACE MENG, New York
LOIS FRANKEL, Florida
TULSI GABBARD, Hawaii
JOAQUIN CASTRO, Texas
ROBIN L. KELLY, Illinois
BRENDAN F. BOYLE, Pennsylvania

AMY PORTER, *Chief of Staff*   THOMAS SHEEHY, *Staff Director*
JASON STEINBAUM, *Democratic Staff Director*

SUBCOMMITTEE ON THE MIDDLE EAST AND NORTH AFRICA

ILEANA ROS-LEHTINEN, Florida, *Chairman*

STEVE CHABOT, Ohio
JOE WILSON, South Carolina
DARRELL E. ISSA, California
RANDY K. WEBER SR., Texas
RON DeSANTIS, Florida
MARK MEADOWS, North Carolina
TED S. YOHO, Florida
CURT CLAWSON, Florida
DAVID A. TROTT, Michigan
LEE M. ZELDIN, New York

THEODORE E. DEUTCH, Florida
GERALD E. CONNOLLY, Virginia
BRIAN HIGGINS, New York
DAVID CICILLINE, Rhode Island
ALAN GRAYSON, Florida
GRACE MENG, New York
LOIS FRANKEL, Florida
BRENDAN F. BOYLE, Pennsylvania

CONTENTS

THE PALESTINIAN AUTHORITY'S INTERNATIONAL CRIMINAL COURT GAMBIT: A TRUE PARTNER FOR PEACE?

WEDNESDAY, FEBRUARY 4, 2015

House of Representatives,
Subcommittee on the Middle East and North Africa,
Committee on Foreign Affairs,
Washington, DC.

The subcommittee met, pursuant to notice, at 2:05 p.m., in room 2172, Rayburn House Office Building, Hon. Ileana Ros-Lehtinen (chairman of the subcommittee) presiding.

Ms. Ros-Lehtinen. The subcommittee will come to order. First, I would like to welcome our new members to the subcommittee. As we begin this new Congress, I look forward to working with my wonderful friend, the ranking member, Mr. Deutch, the returning members of the subcommittee, and our new members, so that we can continue to work in a bipartisan manner to conduct our oversight responsibilities and further advance our foreign policy initiatives and priorities in the region.

After recognizing myself and Ranking Member Deutch for 5 minutes each for our opening statements, I will then recognize any other member seeking recognition for 1 minute.

We will then hear from our witnesses, and without objection, the witnesses' prepared statements will be made a part of the record, and members may have 5 days to insert statements and questions for the record subject to the length limitations in the rules.

I would like to remind audience members that disruption of committee proceedings is against the law and will not be tolerated, although wearing themed shirts while seated in the hearing room is permissible, holding up signs during the proceedings is not. Any disruptions will result in a suspension of the proceedings until the Capitol Police can restore order. And we want you to stay because it is going to be a good hearing. So please don't leave or let yourself be left.

The Chair will now recognize herself for 5 minutes.

In the wake of the administration's failed attempt at achieving an Israeli-Palestinian peace agreement last spring, Abu Mazen and the Palestinian leadership have increased in both intensity and pace their scheme to achieve unilaterally what they have refused to do so directly with the democratic Jewish State of Israel, which is establish an independent state of Palestine. The latest and perhaps most dangerous manifestation of this push was when Abu

(1)

Mazen and the Palestinians acceded to the Rome Statute to join the International Criminal Court after last December's Palestinian-backed U.N. Security Council resolution failed. That the administration was unable to prevent the Palestinian leadership from going to the U.N. and then again to the ICC, underscores the notion that our credibility and leverage have waned so much to the point where our diplomacy efforts end up doing perhaps more harm than good. The situation and these problems perhaps could have been avoided had the administration taken a tougher stance with the PA using the only real leverage that we have, namely the hundreds of millions of dollars that we give each year, instead of coddling it and refusing to cut off the aid, hoping and wishing that Abu Mazen would change his tune.

President Obama should have immediately suspended all aid to the PA once the unity deal between Fatah and Hamas was announced. The letter and the intent of the law is clear: No funding can go to a power-sharing government that includes Hamas or a government that is backed by the terrorist group. Instead, the administration interpreted that the new PA Government was formed in a manner that did not trigger this law. That was a huge mistake, as it once again undermined our ability and credibility on the world stage, only served to encourage Abu Mazen to further challenge the U.S., to further challenge Israel, believing that he had been given the implicit support of the administration.

And now we once again find ourselves in a situation where the administration is refusing to follow the letter and the intent of the law in the wake of the Palestinians joining the ICC and the ICC opening an investigation into Israel over alleged war crimes. The ICC has already shown its overzealousness, which has caused concern. It admitted a non-state party. It is attempting to claim jurisdiction over a non-member state. It has signalled that it is willing to use political determination rather than legal ones, and it is essentially defining Israel's borders and the borders of a non-existent state of Palestine, which is completely beyond its jurisdiction.

U.S. law is clear that should the Palestinians join and initiate or support an investigation into Israel, all funding for the PA must be suspended. Yet the administration not only continued funding, but it requested $370 million for the PA in the President's budget released just 2 days ago. Congress must not allow the President to continue to ignore the letter and the intent of the laws that we pass. Abu Mazen must be held accountable for his actions, and the PLO must be held accountable, and we must also hold the President accountable to uphold the laws.

It is long past time that the administration reassess its policy approach to Israel and the Palestinians. What has resulted since the administration failed to achieve a bilateral agreement between the two parties last spring is a litany of foreign policy failures, one after the other. First, Abu Mazen and PA's ruling party, Fatah, and the designated terrorist group Hamas formed a unity government. Tensions escalated between Gaza and Israel, aided by the incitement from Abu Mazen which led to the brazen kidnapping and brutal murder of three Israeli teens by members of Hamas.

Hamas launched a full rocket attack campaign against Israel which then ultimately resulted in last summer's conflict in Gaza.

Despite this, the administration continues to show its tone-deafness when it comes to the Israelis and the Palestinians. And it is easy to see how its efforts at peace last year actually encouraged Abu Mazen to push forward with his unilateral statehood scheme, which has brought us to where we are today. Yet the administration focuses its time and effort to alienate our ally Israel and has taken unprecedented steps to openly chastise and criticize Israeli leadership in the media. Talk about misplaced priorities and failed diplomacy.

And with that, I am pleased to yield to my friend, the ranking member Mr. Deutch of Florida.

Mr. DEUTCH. Thank you, Chairwoman Ros-Lehtinen, and let me also take just a moment to welcome back the members of this committee and our three new members as well. I would like to note that Chairwoman Ros-Lehtinen and I have worked to make this committee function in a bipartisan way, and while their may be differences of opinion, we appreciate the way the members of this committee have found areas to work together. And we hope that that spirit of bipartisan continues this Congress.

Thanks to our panel for being here. You are familiar faces to this subcommittee, and we welcome you back.

There is no doubt that this hearing comes at an extraordinary time in Israeli-Palestinian relations. After nearly 2 years of dialogue and talks, the peace process is stalled, and we are finally facing what many of us have feared, an effort by the Palestinians to circumvent negotiations altogether.

But achieving a state through unilateral measures has failed, and it will always fail. Nevertheless in a move that will only set back his cause, President Abbas went to the International Criminal Court, and despite U.S. efforts to halt PA's accession, U.N. Secretary General Ban Ki-Moon has announced that the PA will become members of the ICC on April 1. Perhaps more importantly, the PA has already ceded territorial jurisdiction to the ICC, allowing for the initial steps of an investigation. And as we will hear from our witnesses today, the ICC has never undertaken a case like this, and it is unknown if this moves forward, how long an investigation might take and what the implications might be.

This kind of unilateral action is unacceptable. It is an egregious breach of U.S. trust, and despite the repeated warnings of Congress and the administration, despite changes made in U.S. law to respond to these actions, President Abbas chose to take these reckless actions that do nothing to advance peace, nothing to advance peace. And so, in response, I and other senior members of this committee have informed the administration that in the meantime, no new aid to support the PA will be approved. Other strong measures of disfavor will be considered by this committee and by this Congress.

Now let me be clear: I don't want to see the breakdown of cooperation between the PA and Israel. It is in both of their interests to continue strong security cooperation in the West Bank. This coordination prevents terrorist attacks. It leads to the neutralization of Hamas operatives, and it saves innocent Israeli and Palestine lives. The ending of such cooperation could lead to increased violence and attacks on Israel. And I hope that those in the Palestine authority who use a cutoff in security operation as a threat understand the implications of this for their people.

Madam Chairman, so many of us want a genuine peace, a peace with two states for two people. I want to see Israel continue to thrive as a safe and secure democracy, and I would like to see stability and success for the Palestinian people. But the actions that we have seen by President Abbas over the last few months move us further and further from this goal. Longstanding U.N. resolutions, as well as U.S. and Quartet policy, states that lasting peace will only come through direct negotiations. There are hard choices that are going to have to be made on both sides, but simply refusing to negotiate, circumventing the established process, not getting back to the President of the United States to respond to proposals during negotiations, suggests a clear unwillingness to make those hard choices. Israel faces terrorist threats on every one of its borders. Hezbollah is armed with tens of thousands of rockets, and as we saw last week, is willing to attack. Hamas digs tunnels and launches rockets at Israeli civilians. Terrorist in the Sanai launch attacks in the south, not to mention the existential threat of a nuclear-armed Iran. So for those of us who seek peace, we know that Israel's safety and security must never be compromised, which is why many of us here have a hard time understanding why anyone who believes in peace would ever choose to partner in a government with a terrorist organization, one that launched over 3,000 rockets at civilians this summer, one that has never recognized Israel's right to exist, has not recognized even Israel's very right to exist, has never renounced violence, and continues to incite violence on a daily basis.

So what happens next? What are the ramifications if the ICC continues to move forward with an investigation? Well, U.S. law is clear. There will be no aid to the Palestinian Authority, but more broadly, these actions fundamentally have changed the relationship between the United States and the Palestinian Authority. And the question that I have for the panel is, have we reached the place where negotiations are simply out of reach?

And I look forward to hearing from our wonderful group of panelists today, and I yield back.

Ms. ROS-LEHTINEN. Thank you so much, Mr. Deutch.

I know that some of our audience members got here late, so before we proceed, I would like to remind our guests that they must remain seated, and they cannot hold up signs. And I would like to remind audience members that the disruption of committee proceedings is against the law, will not be tolerated.

Although wearing themed shirts while seated in the hearing room is permitted, holding up signs during the proceedings is not. Any disruptions will result in a suspension of the proceedings until Capitol Police can restore order.

We don't want to get anyone in trouble. So please don't make me do that.

Thank you so much.

With that, I would like to recognize the members of our subcommittee for any opening statement they would like to make.

And I will start with Mr. DeSantis.

Mr. DESANTIS. Thank you, Madam Chairman, and you are exactly right: Funding should have stopped the minute that unity government was formed. That is what the law says. I don't think the administration was faithful to that.

It is interesting, you have Hamas and Fatah, they are going to go and accuse Israel of war crimes, and yet they have been conducting terror attacks, suicide attacks, rocket attacks, using human shields. When Israel tries to defend itself, they have consistently violated international law. So it is a curious thing to do. I think the reason that they are doing it is because they see that Israel is under siege by hostile forces, now Hezbollah even more so. And I think this effort is designed to impose political costs on Israel for defending itself against attacks by a group that desire Israel's destruction.

And if you can launch attacks from Gaza, and then when Israel responds, the world blames Israel, then they may not be willing to respond as forcefully as they need to to defend their citizens. So we should call this gambit what it is, and we should respond with the power of the purse.

Ms. ROS-LEHTINEN. Thank you so much, sir.

Mr. Cicilline of Rhode Island.

Mr. CICILLINE. Thank you, Chairman Ros-Lehtinen and Ranking Member Deutch, for calling this timely hearing today.

And thank you to our witnesses for offering your testimony.

We know that lasting peace will only come about as a result of a direct set of negotiations that ultimately lead to a two-state solution. This is the only viable way to resolve the conflict between Israel and the Palestinian people, not through unilateral action. The breakdown of talks led by Secretary Kerry and the subsequent military conflict last summer were extremely disappointing. And the Palestinian decision to form a unity government with Hamas, a terrorist organization, and then to pursue recognition at international institutions, including the ICC, in complete disregard of their agreements made in accordance with the Oslo Peace Accords has seriously jeopardized the possibility of a peaceful solution.

I also fear this move, and the inevitable reaction by Israel and ultimately the United States if a case does move forward, will jeopardize the viability of the Palestinian Authority leading to a dangerous power vacuum in the Palestinian territories.

I look forward to the testimony of our witnesses and hope that we can get some clarity on what this development means for the future of U.S. relations with Israel and the Palestinian Authority.

I thank you, and I yield back.

Ms. ROS-LEHTINEN. Thank you, sir.

Dr. Yoho of Florida.

Mr. YOHO. Thank you, Madam Chair.

I look forward to hearing from the panel with concrete suggestions on how we can change our policy so we don't have this meeting next year talking about the same things. We need a paradigm shift, and I look forward to hearing from you your suggestions so we can implement that and talk about baseball next time you come here.

Ms. ROS-LEHTINEN. Mr. Boyle, one of our new members from Pennsylvania is recognized.

Welcome.

Mr. BOYLE. As a new member, I have to learn to hit the button that says talk.

Thank you, Madam Chair and also Ranking Member Deutch.

I would just briefly say that with the ICC application, something that has happened in the last several months that deeply concerns me is the increase in an effort in the international community to isolate and stigmatize Israel. I am deeply concerned that this latest effort is merely yet another attempt in this long-going campaign, especially by those countries, not the United States, but other countries in Europe and elsewhere that are otherwise allies of the U.S. So I am very interested in what we can do as a country to stand up for Israel, to stand up for human rights of all people, and to ensure that the ICC isn't corrupted and used and abused in a way that is really just about bashing Israel. Thank you.

Ms. ROS-LEHTINEN. Thank you very much and welcome to our subcommittee.

And I apologize to Ms. Meng for skipping her over, but I will get to you.

Curt Clawson of Florida is recognized.

Mr. CLAWSON. Thank you for coming today and sharing your time and expertise, and I really appreciate it, and I am looking forward to what you have to say about security in the region.

You know, as I read about this process, it feels unclear to me that we are going to be more secure tomorrow than we are today on either side of the conflict, and that really is the bottom line. If more people die because of this process, then what are we doing? So I am really interested to hear what you all have to say about everybody's security. There is just too much dying. Thank you.

Ms. ROS-LEHTINEN. Thank you.

Ms. Meng of New York is recognized.

Ms. MENG. Thank you, Madam Chair and Ranking Member Deutch for calling this hearing and our distinguished witnesses for joining us today. In pursuing legal proceedings against Israel in the International Criminal Court, the Palestinian Authority could do irreparable damage to the peace process and escalate the conflict. Furthermore, I am concerned that the PA's actions here contravene both international law and the spirit of existing agreements between Israel and the PA. We must be clear that joining the ICC is not a viable approach for the Palestinians. I look forward to today's testimony, particularly that relating to the legal questions here. I yield back.

Ms. ROS-LEHTINEN. Thank you so much, Ms. Meng.

Mr. Wilson of South Carolina is recognized.

Mr. WILSON. Thank you, Chairwoman Ros-Lehtinen and Ranking Member Deutch, for hosting this important hearing, and thanks to each of our panelists for being here today.

Time and time again the world has seen over 3,000 terrorist rocket attacks which originate from Palestinian-backed terror organization Hamas. As we discuss Palestine's desire to become more integrated within the international community, it should stop terrorism against Israeli women and children. In an effort to bring many of these actions into light, the Web site, Palestinian Media Watch, palwatch.org, does an excellent job of highlighting instances of aggression toward Israel which otherwise may not be told. I support this Web site in its mission.

The U.S. must stand firmly with Israel, our strongest ally in the region. And I fully support Prime Minister Benjamin Netanyahu as he seeks to promote peace in the region.

Ms. ROS-LEHTINEN. Thank you very much.

And with that, I would like to—I don't think Ms. Frankel would like to make a statement, so we will go to Mr. Weber of Texas.

Mr. WEBER. Thank you, Madam Chair. I have been following those events as well, and the gentleman from South Carolina is correct. It seems that the majority, there has been a lot of rockets aimed at Israel. They seem to be going that direction. So those who are crying foul, may indeed be acting the most foul, if I can use that play on words. So I am looking forward to this discussion and see that we do what we can to protect our ally.

Ms. ROS-LEHTINEN. Thank you very much, Mr. Weber.

And we are proud to introduce a new member of our subcommittee, Mr. Zeldin of New York.

Welcome.

Mr. ZELDIN. Thank you, Madam Chairwoman and Ranking Member Deutch, my mother's Congressman, Congressman Deutch. I thank you for holding this hearing today.

And my background before going into elected office was in the military, and first I was a military intelligence officer and then a JAG officer. And in our preparations, whether it is Iraq or Afghanistan or elsewhere, we focus on rules of law, rules of engagement, law of war. We are used to a conventional fight in the past, and we have a doctrine that should be respected when there is war. And the fact that you have Hamas living amongst neighbors, women and children, when you have an important, proportionate response, collateral damage ends up increasing when the threat lives with women and children. And I think that one of the things that we really need to tackle in the dialogue and the conflict between Israel and the conversation with the Palestinian Authority is the unnecessary collateral damage that is taking place. And the Palestinian Authority has a responsibility to route that out from within their ranks, and Israel has a responsibility as well. All of us do, whenever we are engaged in any type of a conflict.

But the amount of collateral damage and civilian deaths taking place across the borders from Israel is a responsibility of the Palestinian Authority to do more for Hamas not to live amongst the ranks of the women and children.

I thank you again, Chairwoman, for doing this hearing.

Ms. ROS-LEHTINEN. Thank you. Welcome.

And Mr. Connolly of Virginia is recognized.

Mr. CONNOLLY. I thank the chair. I am glad to have this panel and this hearing. I just want to say I probably am somewhat demure from some of my colleagues with respect to the necessity of continuing to provide economic development assistance to the Palestinian Authority.

But having said that, Congress did put conditions on that aid last year, and those conditions have to do with the whole question of the ICC. And I know the State Department is reviewing as we speak whether that provision is now triggered. So hopefully we can persuade the Palestinian Authority that unilateral action is not in its best interest, nor ours, and that as we move forward, it has to be in the context of a broader peace negotiation. And I would hope that at this hearing we could illuminate that issue and have more clarity as to what the U.S. policy should be moving forward.

With that, I yield back.

Ms. ROS-LEHTINEN. Thank you, sir.

And now I am pleased to present our panelists. First, I am so happy to welcome back Dr. Jonathan Schanzer, who is the vice president of research for the Foundation for Defense of Democracy. He has written extensively on the Middle East and has chronicled the internal struggle between the PA and Fatah.

Thank you.

Then we welcome Professor Eugene Kontorovich, who is a Professor at Northwestern University School of Law. He has published extensively on the ICC, its jurisdiction, and the court's legal basis. The professor has been cited on leading international law cases around the world, and he is a regular contributor to the Washington Post.

Welcome, Professor.

And, third, we welcome back Ms. Danielle Pletka. She is the senior vice president for foreign and defense policy studies at the American Institute. She served for 10 years as a senior professional staff member for the Near East and South Asia Subcommittee on the Senate Foreign Relations Committee.

I don't know. Mr. Connolly, perhaps you served with her. Were you a Senate staffer?

Mr. CONNOLLY. I probably did.

Ms. ROS-LEHTINEN. Might have.

And, finally, we welcome back David Makovsky. He is a distinguished fellow and director of the Project on the Middle East Peace Process at the Washington Institute. David is the author of numerous research pieces on the Arab-Israel conflict and has just concluded a 10-month stint as Senior Advisor to Secretary of State Kerry's Israeli-Palestine Peace Talks Team.

Welcome all of the panelists. Your written statements will be made a part of the record, and we will start with you, sir.

STATEMENT OF JONATHAN SCHANZER, PH.D., VICE PRESIDENT FOR RESEARCH, FOUNDATION FOR DEFENSE OF DEMOCRACIES

Mr. SCHANZER. Chairman Ros-Lehtinen, Ranking Member Deutch, members of the committee. On behalf of FDD, thank you for inviting me to testify today.

After a decade of lobbying the international community for recognition at the U.N., the Palestinians are now poised to leverage their gains and wage lawfare at the International Criminal Court. The goal for Palestinian President Mahmoud Abbas has been the same since he launched his diplomatic campaign in 2005, and that is to force the Israelis to relinquish territory or other meaningful concessions and to do so outside the scope of bilateral negotiations.

The dangers of this campaign cannot be understated. For one, these efforts are not likely to resolve the conflict peacefully. Rather, they will keep the embers of conflict glowing. More importantly, while communication and cooperation still exist between Ramallah and Washington, it is clear that Abbas and his lieutenants no longer feel beholden to the United States despite the hundreds of millions of dollars in assistance we provide every year.

Madam Chairman, threats to cut assistance to the Palestinian Authority have not had the desired impact in recent years. The reason for this is simple. Washington is dependent upon the PA for continued security cooperation with Israel. Abbas knows this, and this is why he feels comfortable testing the patience of legislators and the President.

There are, however, steps that we can take to reassert American leverage in the West Bank, protect American interests, empower new moderate Palestinian leadership, and safeguard Israeli security concerns.

First, Congress should strongly consider establishing a lawfare office similar to that established by Israel. Such an office can help the U.S. Government battle lawfare against us in both defense of U.S. officials and perhaps even our allies as well. Along these lines, we can leverage our Article 98 agreements with foreign governments. The U.S. Government already has about 100 of these agreements which ensure that U.S. persons are not surrendered to the jurisdiction of the ICC. Congress should ensure that the U.S. enters into as many of these agreements as possible and perhaps even modify them to include its key allies, such as Israel.

In the meantime, we have to deter the Palestinians from their current course. One way to do that is to work with our intelligence community to declassify information about Palestine terrorism, illicit activity, and human rights abuses dating back to November 29, 2012, when the U.N. General Assembly recognized Palestine as a non-member observer state. This would send a message to the Palestine leadership that it is just as susceptible, if not more so, to ICC prosecution.

Congress must also take steps to weaken the PLO. It is the PLO that is pursuing Israel at the ICC, and it is the PLO that is waging the diplomatic campaign at the U.N. Moreover, the PLO still has terrorist groups under its umbrella. Its leaders are unelected. Its decisionmaking is opaque, and its finances are obscured from the public eye. Its very existence enables a dysfunctional system. At any given time, we don't know whether it is the PLO, the Fatah faction, or the PA that is speaking in the Palestinians' in the name. If the goal is to hold the Palestinian leadership responsible for its actions, it is time to empower the Palestinian Government we seek to engage and to make the PLO obsolete. To that end we must shut down the PLO Embassy in Washington and to take steps to weaken the organization worldwide.

In addition, we should make plans for Mahmoud Abbas to go. He is a huge part of the problem. Once considered a reformer, he is now 10 years into a 5-year Presidential term. He is the head of the Fatah faction and the PLO. So long as he maintains a stranglehold over the Palestinian political system, the Palestinians will be taken in by gimmicks like the U.N. recognition campaign and the ICC. We have to begin to plan for new elections.

However, we cannot only focus on the West Bank political structures. The Hamas-Fatah split remains a challenge that will encumber both regional peace and Palestinian reform. Hamas must be removed from the Gaza Strip and from the political process if change is to take root.

Finally, Washington must return to its role as arbiter of the peace process. I don't believe that peace between the current leaders is likely, nor do I believe that this administration has earned the trust of either side. However, Washington cannot abdicate its role as the honest broker. Once we return to that role, we will have an opportunity to call for a halt to all unilateral action and guide this conflict to a more constructive dynamic.

Thank you for the opportunity to testify today, and I look forward to answering your questions.

Ms. ROS-LEHTINEN. Thank you so much.

[The prepared statement of Mr. Schanzer follows:]

Congressional Testimony

The Palestinian Authority's International Criminal Court Gambit: A True Partner for Peace?

Jonathan Schanzer
Vice President for Research
Foundation for Defense of Democracies

**Hearing before the
House Foreign Affairs Committee
Subcommittee on the Middle East and North Africa**

Washington, DC
February 4, 2015

FDD
FOUNDATION FOR
DEFENSE OF DEMOCRACIES

1726 M Street NW • Suite 700 • Washington, DC 20036

Chairman Ros-Lehtinen, Ranking Member Deutch, members of the Committee, on behalf of the Foundation for Defense of Democracies (FDD), thank you for inviting me to testify today.

After a decade of successful efforts to gain support from the international community for recognition of statehood, the Palestinians are now poised to leverage their gains and wage lawfare at the International Criminal Court (ICC). The goal for Palestinian president Mahmoud Abbas has been the same throughout this campaign: to force the Israelis to relinquish territory or other meaningful concessions, and to do so outside the scope of bilateral negotiations.

The dangers of this campaign cannot be understated. For one, these efforts are not likely to resolve the conflict peacefully. Rather, they will keep the embers of conflict glowing. More importantly, eschewing both the U.S. leadership and the bilateral diplomatic process reflects a troubling trend. While communication and cooperation still exists between Ramallah and Washington, it is clear that Abbas and his lieutenants no longer feel beholden to the United States, despite the hundreds of millions of dollars in assistance we provide every year. We must find ways of regaining our leverage in the West Bank, and to do so without undermining stability in the Middle East.

As I explain at the end of this testimony, Washington needs to construct a strategy to combat lawfare, both against America and its allies. We must also hold to account those responsible for this reckless initiative: Mahmoud Abbas and the Palestine Liberation Organization (PLO).

"PALESTINE 194"

Before expanding on my recommendations, it is important to review the history of the Palestinian international initiative. Indeed, the ICC bid is just the latest manifestation—perhaps the culmination—of a campaign the Palestinians have waged for ten years. Palestinian officials call it "Palestine 194," shorthand for their push to become the 194th state at the United Nations.

It all began when newly elected president Mahmoud Abbas traveled to Brazil in 2005 for the first Summit of South American and Arab States, where he had a private conversation with Brazil's president, Luiz Inácio Lula da Silva. Da Silva reportedly promised Abbas that he would lay the groundwork to gain Latin American support for a future Palestinian statehood declaration at the United Nations.[1] In the coming years, da Silva made good on his pledge. In 2008, Costa Rica officially recognized a Palestinian state.[2] In 2009, Venezuela followed suit as the Palestinians opened an embassy in Caracas.[3] In 2010, Argentina, Bolivia, and Ecuador all expressed their support for a Palestinian state within the 1967 borders.[4] More Latin American countries soon

---

[1] Jonathan Schanzer, *State of Failure*, (New York: Palgrave Macmillan, 2013), page 174.
[2] "United Nations Latin American and Caribbean Meeting in Support of Israel-Palestinian Peace Concludes in Montevideo, Uruguay," *United Nations*, March 31, 2011.
(http://www.un.org/News/Press/docs/2011/gapal1193.doc.htm)
[3] "Venezuelan-Palestinian Ties Forged," *Al-Jazeera* (Qatar), April 28, 2009.
(http://www.aljazeera.com/news/americas/2009/04/2009427234224190396.html)
[4] "Brazil, Argentina, Uruguay Recognize Palestinian State," *Agence France Presse*, December 6, 2010.
(http://www.google.com/hostednews/afp/article/ALeqM5j6LW4hivgKRMW-N8S1xV6P9AwVew)

joined the parade, including Chile, Guyana, Peru, Paraguay, Suriname, and Uruguay.[5] By 2011, more than a hundred countries had recognized an independent Palestine, and momentum was on their side.[6] And Abbas made it clear that he had a plan. In May 2011, he penned an op-ed in *The New York Times*, in which he stated, "Palestine's admission to the United Nations would pave the way for the internationalization of the conflict as a legal matter, not only a political one. It would also pave the way for us to pursue claims against Israel at the United Nations, human rights treaty bodies and the International Court of Justice."[7]

The ICC, while not mentioned specifically, was never far from the minds of the Palestinian leadership. After Operation Cast Lead in early 2009, the Palestinians began threatening to bring action against Israel at the ICC for war crimes. Shortly after the war, the Palestinian Authority (PA) Minister of Justice lodged an ad-hoc declaration with the ICC seeking jurisdiction to investigate Israeli actions taken during the operation.[8] The ICC sat on this complaint for three years while it deliberated whether or not the Palestinians qualified for ICC jurisdiction. Finally, in 2012, ICC chief prosecutor Luis Moreno-Ocampo rejected the complaint on the grounds that the Palestinians were not an accepted "state" in the international community.[9]

This was a technicality that the Palestinians were already working to change. In the fall of 2011, the Palestinians announced that they would seek recognition as a state at the U.N. Security Council. When it became clear that the Palestinians would not have the necessary support to force a U.S. veto, however, the Palestinians called off the vote.[10] Instead, they recalculated their strategy and decided to push for a vote at the U.N. General Assembly the following year. While the General Assembly could not grant them official statehood, it could gain them standing at the ICC. The General Assembly was undeniably the path of least resistance; the Palestinians had successfully lobbied for the support of a majority of the member nations, and the U.S. has no veto in the General Assembly. Predictably, the Palestinians easily sailed through a 138 to 9 vote in favor of upgrading their status to non-member observer state.[11]

[5] "Peru Recognizes Palestinian State," *Reuters*, January 24, 2011. (http://www.reuters.com/article/2011/01/24/us-palestinians-peru-idUSTRE70N5ZW20110124); "Paraguay Recognizes 'Palestine' with Pre-1967 Borders," *The Jerusalem Post*, January 29, 2011. (http://www.jpost.com/International/Article.aspx?id=205690); "Guyana Becomes 7th South American State to Recognize Palestinian Independence," *Haaretz* (Israel), January 14, 2011. (http://www.haaretz.com/news/diplomacy-defense/guyana-becomes-7th-south-american-state-to-recognize-palestinian-independence-1.336944); "Suriname Recognizes Palestinian State," *Ma'an News Agency* (Palestinian Territories), February 1, 2011. (http://www.maannews.net/eng/ViewDetails.aspx?ID=356264); & "Uruguay Recognizes Palestinian State," *Reuters*, March 15, 2011. (http://ca.reuters.com/article/topNews/idCATRE72F0SA20110316)

[6] Jonathan Schanzer, *State of Failure*, (New York: Palgrave Macmillan, 2013), page 176.

[7] Mahmoud Abbas, "The Long Overdue Palestinian State," *The New York Times*. May 16, 2011. (http://www.nytimes.com/2011/05/17/opinion/17abbas.html)

[8] Victor Kattan, "Palestine and the International Criminal Court," *European Council on Foreign Relations*, September 1, 2014. (http://www.ecfr.eu/article/commentary_palestine_and_the_international_criminal_court303)

[9] Marlise Simons, "Court Rejects Palestinians in Their Bid for a Tribunal," *The New York Times*, April 3, 2012. (http://www.nytimes.com/2012/04/04/world/middleeast/international-criminal-court-rejects-palestinian-bid-for-tribunal.html)

[10] Chris McGreal, "UN Vote on Palestinian State Put Off Amid Lack of Support," *The Guardian* (U.K.), November 11. 2011. (http://www.theguardian.com/world/2011/nov/11/united-nations-delays-palestinian-statehood-vote)

[11] Ethan Bronner & Christine Hauser, "U.N. Assembly, in Blow to U.S., Elevates Status of Palestine," *The New York Times*, November 29, 2012. (http://www.nytimes.com/2012/11/30/world/middleeast/Palestinian-Authority-United-Nations-Israel.html?pagewanted=all&_r=0)

In the months that followed the 2012 vote, the Palestinians paid a political price. Israel withheld tax revenues, the U.S. condemned the maneuver, and the political upheaval in Ramallah over the move led to the resignation of Prime Minister Salaam Fayyad.[12] Fayyad believed that Abbas was putting the cart before the horse, focusing on the trappings of statehood, while failing to focus on the basic governance and bureaucratic needs of the fledgling government.[13]

With Fayyad out of the picture, Abbas pushed on. In June 2013, Abbas evoked the "successes" of the Palestine 194 campaign at a speech in Ramallah, vowing, "These steps will be followed by others."[14] Shortly thereafter, the new chief prosecutor of the ICC, Fatou Bensouda, announced that the Palestinians were eligible to join the ICC owing to their upgraded status at the U.N. General Assembly.[15] Palestinian officials used her announcement as a means to threaten Israel, stating that unless Israel met their demands, they would turn to the ICC.[16]

DIPLOMACY, UNITY, AND WAR

With diplomatic tensions rising, Secretary of State John Kerry stepped in and announced the resumption of diplomatic negotiations. One of his preconditions for the talks was that the Palestinians halt the 194 campaign. Indeed, preventing the advance of the 194 campaign was among the reasons for launching this new peace process. Reluctantly, the Palestinians agreed to put their efforts on ice while the talks took place.[17]

However, it was a promise they would not keep. Abbas came under significant pressure from some of his own allies who believed the 194 campaign was the only way to extract concessions from Israel. Notably, Mohammad Shtayyeh, one of the chief architects of the Palestinian bid at the Security Council, pressured the beleaguered president to re-launch the campaign.[18]

---

[12] Isabel Kershner, "Israel to Transfer Tax Funds to Palestinians," *The New York Times*, January 30, 2013. (http://www.nytimes.com/2013/01/31/world/middleeast/israel-to-transfer-tax-funds-to-palestinians.html); & Isabel Kershner & Jodi Rudoren, "Palestinian Prime Minister Resigns, Adding Uncertainty to Government," *The New York Times*, April 13, 2013. (http://www.nytimes.com/2013/04/14/world/middleeast/salam-fayyad-palestinian-prime-minister-resigns.html?pagewanted=all)

[13] "After Fayyad," *Chicago Tribune*, April 21, 2013, (http://articles.chicagotribune.com/2013-04-21/opinion/ct-edit-fayyad-20130420_1_fayyadism-corruption-moribund-palestinian-economy)

[14] "Abbas: Palestinians Will Never Give Up on Jerusalem," *Wafa News Agency* (Palestinian Territories), June 5, 2013. (http://english.wafa.ps/index.php?action=detail&id=22561)

[15] "Prosecutor: Palestine Could Join ICC," *Ma'an News Agency* (Palestinian Territories), June 22, 2013. (http://www.maannews.net/eng/ViewDetails.aspx?ID=607163)

[16] Grant Rumley, "Palestine's Plan B," *The National Interest*, July 30, 2013. (http://nationalinterest.org/commentary/palestines-plan-b-8792)

[17] Ben Birnbaum & Amir Tibon, "The Explosive, Inside Story of How John Kerry Built an Israel-Palestine Peace Plan—and Watched It Crumble," *The New Republic*, July 20, 2014. (http://www.newrepublic.com/article/118751/how-israel-palestine-peace-deal-died)

[18] David Lerman & Nicole Gaouette, "Mideast Peace Deal is a Fading Mirage as Palestinians Turn to UN," *Bloomberg*, January 5, 2015. (http://www.bloomberg.com/news/2015-01-05/mideast-peace-deal-is-a-fading-mirage-as-palestinians-turn-to-un.html)

According to one account, the internal pressure campaign, coupled with a marked lack of diplomatic progress, began to take a toll on Abbas in March 2014.[19]

In meetings in Washington with both President Obama and Secretary Kerry, it became clear that Abbas had lost faith in the American diplomatic effort.[20] Abbas wanted Israel to release a fourth batch of Palestinian prisoners, which had been a precondition at the start of the talks. After three other swaps, the Israelis were now reticent to follow through. Abbas's calculation ultimately boiled down to this: if the U.S. couldn't get concessions out of Israel, perhaps the international community could.[21]

The next month, Abbas effectively dissolved the Kerry talks when he announced that the Palestinians would join 15 international organizations and conventions.[22] The move had little practical impact—the organizations and conventions were relatively innocuous in that they provided little ammunition for the Palestinians' legal assault against Israel—but it was a means to convey to the United States and Israel that the international campaign was back in play. More importantly, Palestinian officials warned Western journalists and academics that this first tranche represented a step in the direction of joining the ICC.[23]

The implication was that the Palestinians would press for action against Israel for building settlements in territory the Palestinians claim for their national project—activity they say is a war crime.[24] Indeed, Palestinian officials routinely pointed to Israel's settlements in the West Bank as a violation of international law. As PA Foreign Minister Riyad al-Maliki noted, "If Israel would like to go further by implementing the E1 [settlement] plan and the other related plans around Jerusalem then yes, we will be going to the ICC."[25]

Along with jumpstarting the international campaign for recognition, Abbas also took the dangerous step of forging a unity government with the terrorist group Hamas on June 2, 2014.[26]

[19] Ben Birnbaum & Amir Tibon, "The Explosive, Inside Story of How John Kerry Built an Israel-Palestine Peace Plan—And Watched it Crumble," *The New Republic*, July 20, 2014. (http://www.newrepublic.com/article/118751/how-israel-palestine-peace-deal-died)

[20] Michael Wilner, "At White House, Abbas Says Israel's Recognition is Settled," *The Jerusalem Post*, March 17, 2014. (http://www.jpost.com/Diplomacy-and-Politics/Abbas-to-Obama-Time-is-not-on-our-side-for-two-state-solution-345624)

[21] Ben Birnbaum & Amir Tibon, "The Explosive, Inside Story of How John Kerry Built an Israel-Palestine Peace Plan—And Watched it Crumble," *The New Republic*, July 20, 2014. (http://www.newrepublic.com/article/118751/how-israel-palestine-peace-deal-died)

[22] Grant Rumley, "Suicide by Statehood," *Foreign Policy*, April 2, 2014. (http://foreignpolicy.com/2014/04/02/suicide-by-statehood/)

[23] Grant Rumley, "Palestine's Plan B," *The National Interest*, July 30, 2013. (http://nationalinterest.org/commentary/palestines-plan-b-8792)

[24] Eugene Kontorovich, "Palestinians Seek to Take Advantage of ICC's Unique 'Israel' Provision," *The Washington Post*, January 5, 2015. (http://www.washingtonpost.com/news/volokh-conspiracy/wp/2015/01/05/palestinians-seek-to-take-advantage-of-iccs-unique-israel-provision/)

[25] Louis Charbonneau, "Palestinians Say They May Have No Choice But to Take Israel to Hague Court," *Reuters*, January 23, 2013. (http://www.reuters.com/article/2013/01/23/us-palestinians-israel-un-idUSBRE90M1EX20130123)

[26] William Booth & Anne Gearan, "Palestinians Form New Unity Government that Includes Hamas," *The Washington Post*, June 2, 2014. (http://www.washingtonpost.com/world/middle_east/palestinians-form-new-unity-government-including-hamas/2014/06/02/c681d5c6-ea46-11e3-9f5c-9075d5508f0a_story.html)

This was perhaps the clearest signal to the Israelis and the United States that he was no longer interested in negotiating. Indeed, he knew that the Israelis would never negotiate with him so long as Hamas was in the picture, given Hamas' stated aim of destroying the Jewish state. Under fire from the U.S. and Israel, Palestinian officials insisted the new interim government was one made up only of technocrats that would serve as caretakers until elections were held.[27]

That move, coupled with Hamas's kidnapping and murder of three teens in the West Bank in late June, put the region on a war footing.[28] The Israelis' frantic search for the three youths[29] and the murder of a Palestinian teen by a mentally ill Israeli[30] paved the way for a 50-day war between Israel and Hamas. During the conflict, Hamas fired 4,564 rockets into Israeli airspace, prompting Israeli air strikes and a limited ground invasion to destroy commando tunnels and other military infrastructure.[31] The fighting claimed the lives of 2,104 Palestinians and 72 Israelis.[32]

From the onset of the clashes in July, it was clear that the Palestinian Authority's strategy was to refrain from the fight, even as it prepared to charge the Israelis with war crimes. One day after the Israelis launched Operation Protective Edge, Abbas claimed that Israel was committing "genocide."[33] Ten days into the fighting, Riyad Mansour, the Palestinian ambassador to the U.N., threatened to go to "judicial bodies" should the U.N. fail to protect Palestinian citizens in Gaza. "We will have no recourse but to turn to the judicial bodies of the United Nations and the international system," he said.[34]

Lawyers also began making the case for Israeli war crimes, including here in the United States, well before the war was over.[35] The most high profile among them was a French lawyer who lodged a complaint in late July at the International Criminal Court on behalf of the Palestinian justice minister, accusing the Israeli army of war crimes. "Israel, the occupying power, is

---

[27] "Palestinian Authority to Start Formation of Technocratic Unity Government," *Middle East Monitor*, April 24. 2014. (https://www.middleeastmonitor.com/news/middle-east/11067-palestinian-authority-to-start-formation-of-technocratic-unity-government)

[28] Orlando Crowcroft, "Hamas Official: We Were Behind the Kidnapping of Three Israeli Teenagers," *The Guardian* (U.K.), August 21, 2014. (http://www.theguardian.com/world/2014/aug/21/hamas-kidnapping-three-israeli-teenagers-saleh-al-arouri-qassam-brigades)

[29] "Israel Arrests 37 in West Bank as Manhunt Drags On," *The National* (UAE), June 23, 2014. (http://www.thenational.ae/world/middle-east/israel-arrests-37-in-west-bank-as-manhunt-drags-on)

[30] Marissa Newman, "3 Suspects Indicted in Killing of Muhammad Abu Khdeir," *The Times of Israel*, July 17, 2014. (http://www.timesofisrael.com/3-suspects-indicted-in-killing-of-muhammad-abu-khdeir/)

[31] Ben Hartman, "50 Days of Israel's Gaza Operation, Protective Edge – By the Numbers," *The Jerusalem Post*, August 28, 2014. (http://www.jpost.com/Operation-Protective-Edge/50-days-of-Israels-Gaza-operation-Protective-Edge-by-the-numbers-372574)

[32] "Gaza Crisis: Toll of Operations in Gaza," *BBC*, September 1, 2014. (http://www.bbc.com/news/world-middle-east-28439404)

[33] "Abbas Says Israel Committing 'Genocide' in Gaza," *Agence France Presse*, July 9, 2014. (http://www.maannews.net/eng/ViewDetails.aspx?ID=711480)

[34] "Statement by Ambassador Dr. Riyad Mansour Before the United Nations Security Council, Emergency Meeting," *Permanent Observer Mission of the State of Palestine to the United Nations*, July 18, 2014. (http://palestineun.org/18-july-2014-statement-by-ambassador-dr-riyad-mansour-before-the-united-nations-security-council-emergency-meeting/)

[35] Manal Tellawi, "'They Were War Crimes': The Specific, Legal Case for International Charges against Israel," *Salon*, August 4, 2014. (http://www.salon.com/2014/08/04/they_were_war_crimes_the_specific_legal_case_for_international_charges_against_israel/)

carrying out a military operation which in principle and form violates the basis of international law," the lawyer claimed.[36]

In late July, Palestinian media reported that the Palestinian leadership had decided to sign the Rome Statute and pursue the Israelis at the ICC.[37] This proved to be untrue. Subsequent reports indicate that the ICC had yet to receive a nod from the Palestinian Authority to pursue the matter. In an email, ICC chief prosecutor Fatou Bensouda said that the Palestinian leadership had not granted her office jurisdiction to investigate alleged war crimes.[38]

This did not stop others from making such charges, however. One month after the war ended, Human Rights Watch accused Israel of war crimes, citing attacks on three U.N.-run schools that resulted in Palestinian casualties. The Israeli military said during the conflict that Palestinian fighters used the schools as cover to launch rockets.[39] Amnesty International joined the chorus, alleging that the Israel Defense Forces (IDF) destroyed buildings on purpose and without military justification.[40]

POST-WAR MANUEVERS

From the perspective of the Palestinian leadership in Ramallah, the Israeli war against their political foes in Gaza represented new opportunities. For one, it weakened Hamas both militarily and politically. When the guns fell silent, the PA wasted little time reasserting itself as both the leaders of the caretaker unity government and the trusted non-militant faction that could oversee Gaza reconstruction.[41] This enabled the PA to once again claim sovereignty over Gaza and project leadership after 50 days of taking a back seat to its political rivals.

The Ramallah leadership also used the war as a predicate for a renewed push at the United Nations. In August, the head of Fatah's Foreign Relations Committee, Nabil Sha'ath, laid out the roadmap for the Palestinians. They would first look to submit a resolution to the U.N. Security Council demanding a timeframe for a full Israeli withdrawal from beyond the 1967 lines, and should that fail, they would apply for accession to the ICC.[42] A few weeks later, Hamas's prime

---

[36] "Palestinian Minister Goes to ICC Over Israel Offensive," *Agence France Presse*, July 25, 2014. (http://www.maannews.net/eng/ViewDetails.aspx?ID=716175)

[37] "PA to Sign Rome Statute of ICC." *The Times of Israel*, July 31, 2014. (http://www.timesofisrael.com/pa-to-sign-rome-statute-of-international-criminal-court/)

[38] "Is the PA Stalling Gaza War Crimes Probe?" *Al Jazeera* (Qatar), September 12, 2014. (http://www.aljazeera.com/news/middleeast/2014/09/pa-leadership-speaking-with-two-voices-201491101131329372.html)

[39] "Human Rights Watch Accuses Israel of War Crimes in Gaza," *Reuters*, September 11, 2014. (http://www.reuters.com/article/2014/09/11/us-mideast-gaza-war-idUSKBN0H60XZ20140911)

[40] Yonah Jeremy Bob, "Amnesty International: Strikes on Gaza High-Rises Amount to War Crimes," *The Jerusalem Post*, September 12, 2014, (http://www.jpost.com/Arab-Israeli-Conflict/Amnesty-International-Strikes-on-Gaza-high-rises-amount-to-war-crimes-384086)

[41] Jodi Rudoren, "Rival Palestinian Factions Agree to Resolve Differences, Leaders Say," *The New York Times*, September 25, 2014. (http://www.nytimes.com/2014/09/26/world/middleeast/palestinian-factions-agree-to-resolve-differences-leaders-say.html?_r=0)

[42] "PLO to Pursue Diplomatic Efforts Following Ceasefire Deal," *Ma'an News Agency* (Palestinian Territories), August 28, 2014. (http://www.maannews.net/eng/ViewDetails.aspx?ID=723892)

minister, Ismail Haniyeh, called on Abbas to sign the Rome Statute.[43] Abbas now had the blessings of the major Palestinian factions—including Hamas—to accede to the ICC.[44]

With a speech planned at the U.N. General Assembly in September, Abbas was reportedly mulling an ICC application.[45] The speech itself read like a legal incrimination of the Israelis. "This last war against Gaza was a series of absolute war crimes carried out before the eyes and ears of the entire world, moment by moment, in a manner that makes it inconceivable that anyone today can claim that they did not realize the magnitude and horror of the crime," he proclaimed.[46] However, he stopped short of taking his case to the ICC at that time.

In October, the Ramallah leadership released a copy of their draft resolution for the U.N. Security Council. The resolution called for a total Israeli withdrawal from the West Bank and East Jerusalem by November 2016, and for all parties to "abide by their obligations under international humanitarian law."[47] The Israelis promptly condemned the resolution, and Israeli Prime Minister Benjamin Netanyahu warned that if Abbas chose to pursue the U.N. and then the ICC, he would face "dire consequences."[48]

PALESTINE 194 MEETS THE ICC

Netanyahu's threats apparently fell on deaf ears. In December 2014, Ramallah upgraded its status at the ICC to become an observer. This status granted the Palestinians the ability to ratify the Rome Statute while also keeping them out of the court's jurisdiction.[49] By the end of the year, they combined this move with the "Palestine 194" campaign by forwarding a new resolution for statehood to the U.N. Security Council.

The resolution, itself, was not a surprise. The Palestinian leadership had made no secret of the fact that they were circulating a draft and seeking input from the members of the Security Council, the Arab League, and others. However, when it became clear that the Palestinians were likely to lose the vote again, they adopted a more aggressive version with sharper language that

---

[43] "Haniyeh: Weapons of the Resistance are Outside of Any Agreement," *Ma'an News Agency* (Palestinian Territories), September 5, 2014. (http://www.maannews.net/arb/ViewDetails.aspx?ID=725620)

[44] "Abbas Said Close to Deciding on ICC War Crimes Probe," *The Times of Israel*, September 22, 2014. (http://www.timesofisrael.com/abbas-said-close-to-deciding-on-icc-war-crimes-probe/?utm_source=dlvr.it&utm_medium=twitter)

[45] "Abbas Said Close to Deciding on ICC War Crimes Probe," *The Times of Israel*, September 22, 2014. (http://www.timesofisrael.com/abbas-said-close-to-deciding-on-icc-war-crimes-probe/?utm_source=dlvr.it&utm_medium=twitter)

[46] "Palestinian Authority President Abbas' Address to the UN General Assembly in New York," *The Jerusalem Post*, September 26, 2014. (http://www.jpost.com/Middle-East/Full-text-of-Palestinian-Authority-President-Abbas-address-to-the-UN-General-Assembly-in-New-York-376388)

[47] Jack Moore, "UN Draft Resolution Demands End of Israeli Occupation of Palestine by November 2016," *The International Business Times*, October 1, 2014. (http://www.ibtimes.co.uk/un-draft-resolution-demands-end-israeli-occupation-palestine-by-november-2016-1468112)

[48] "Netanyahu: No Chance for Peace Deal if Israel Sued for War Crimes," *Jewish Telegraph Agency*, October 3, 2014. (http://www.jta.org/2014/10/03/news-opinion/israel-middle-east/netanyahu-no-chance-for-peace-deal-if-israel-sued-for-war-crimes)

[49] Somini Sengupta, "Palestinians Become Observers at Meeting on International Criminal Court," *The New York Times*, December 8, 2014. (http://www.nytimes.com/2014/12/09/world/middleeast/palestinians-become-observers-at-meeting-on-international-criminal-court.html?_r=0)

demanded a one-year deadline for negotiations to resume, a full Israeli withdrawal from the West Bank by 2017, and a Palestinian capital in east Jerusalem.[50] The resolution, which was called for hastily on December 30, was defeated. The Palestinians failed to muster the nine votes necessary to pass, instead garnering eight.[51] Had the motion gained the nine votes, the United States (which voted against the motion[52]) was poised to exercise its veto.[53]

One day after the defeat, Abbas announced he had signed the Palestinians' applications to several international conventions and bodies, including the Rome Statute of the ICC.[54] The U.N. acknowledged it received the applications, and Secretary General Ban Ki-Moon confirmed in early January that the Palestinians would become full members of the ICC on April 1, 2015.[55]

The Palestinians had warned that if their Security Council resolution failed, they would turn to the ICC. But few observers understood how quickly they would do so. They have now prompted a process at the ICC of "examining the information available in order to reach a fully informed determination on whether there is a reasonable basis to proceed with an investigation." The investigators are limited to reviewing actions taken since June 2014—the events leading up to the Gaza War (including the kidnapping of the three Israeli teens), the war itself, and presumably any other IDF actions in the West Bank or Gaza subsequent to the conflict.[56] However, the ICC probe can be expanded, dating back to when the Palestinians gained recognition at the General Assembly, on November 29, 2012.[57]

Recently, Mahmoud Abbas told reporters in Cairo that he would consider halting the ICC push should a new round of negotiations be launched soon.[58] But at a recent meeting with Turkish President Recep Tayyip Erdoğan, he vowed to pursue the "Palestine 194" campaign and the ICC in tandem.[59] This has long been the Palestinian strategy, and there is no reason to believe that it will change any time soon without a change in Washington's policies.

---

[50] Michael Gordon & Somini Sengupta, "Resolution for Palestinian State Fails in United Nations Security Council," *The New York Times,* December 30, 2014. (http://www.nytimes.com/2014/12/31/world/middleeast/resolution-for-palestinian-state-fails-in-security-council.html)

[51] Lorenzo Ferrigno, "Security Council Rejects Palestinian Statehood Resolution," *CNN,* December 30, 2014. (http://www.cnn.com/2014/12/30/world/palestinian-statehood-draft-vote/)

[52] Michael Gordon & Somini Sengupta, "Resolution for Palestinian State Fails in United Nations Security Council," *The New York Times,* December 30, 2014. (http://www.nytimes.com/2014/12/31/world/middleeast/resolution-for-palestinian-state-fails-in-security-council.html)

[53] Marissa Newman, "Kerry Said to Hint at Sanctions If Palestinians Push UN Bid," *The Times of Israel,* December 29, 2014. (http://www.timesofisrael.com/kerry-said-to-hint-at-sanctions-if-palestinians-push-un-bid/)

[54] Peter Beaumont, "Palestinian President Signs Up to Join International Criminal Court," *The Guardian* (U.K.), December 31. 2014. (http://www.theguardian.com/world/2014/dec/31/palestinian-president-international-criminal-court)

[55] Yonah Jeremy Bob, "Ban Ki-Moon Says Palestine to Join ICC on April 1," *The Jerusalem Post,* January 7, 2015. (http://www.jpost.com/Arab-Israeli-Conflict/Ban-Ki-moon-says-Palestine-to-join-ICC-on-April-1-386958)

[56] "Israel-Palestinian 'War Crimes' Probed By the ICC," *BBC,* January 16, 2015. (http://www.bbc.com/news/world-middle-east-30851121)

[57] Yonah Jeremy Bob, "Analysis: Palestinians May Face 2012 Cut-Off at ICC," *The Jerusalem Post,* April 4, 2014. (http://www.jpost.com/International/Analysis-Palestinians-may-face-2012-cut-off-at-ICC-347508)

[58] Moshe Cohen, "Report: Abbas 'Willing' to Give Israel a Break on ICC," *Arutz Sheva* (Israel), January 15, 2015. (http://www.israelnationalnews.com/News/News.aspx/189985#.VL_6gUfF9ps)

[59] "Abbas Says Palestinians to Submit New Statehood Bid 'Soon'," *The Times of Israel,* January 12, 2015. (http://www.timesofisrael.com/abbas-says-palestinians-to-submit-new-statehood-bid-soon/)

OPPOSITION FROM WASHINGTON AND JERUSALEM

The response from Israel has been predictably hostile. As Netanyahu stated, "Israel rejects the absurd decision of the ICC prosecutor ... to go after Israel. It's absurd for the ICC to ignore international law and agreements, under which the Palestinians don't have a state and can only get one through direct negotiations with Israel." In other words, Israel objects to both the 194 campaign and the ICC bid because both are violations of the Oslo Accords. The Israelis argue that the Palestinians are looking to force conditions for a Palestinian state on the Israelis rather than achieving a state through negotiations.[60]

In response to the Palestinian ICC bid, the Israelis took the step of freezing the next monthly transfer of tax revenue, which Israel collects on behalf of the PA, totaling some $125 million.[61] Israel's response will also likely include the mobilization of a special office, established in 2009 within Israel's Ministry of Justice, to handle all lawfare issues, including "all international legal proceedings against Israel, Israeli soldiers or officials."[62] To that end, Israel is reportedly mulling a counteroffensive, including a "large-scale prosecution in the United States and elsewhere" of Abbas and other Palestinian officials.[63] It is unclear whether their partnership with Hamas in the unity government is the principal basis for the complaint, or if the Israelis have other plans.

The U.S., for its part, opposed the bid on both sides of the political aisle. President Obama assured Netanyahu that the U.S. and Israel were united in their opposition to Palestinian accession to the ICC.[64] Legislators from both parties have also condemned the ICC bid. Notably, 75 senators recently sent a letter to Secretary of State John Kerry, calling for a cut in aid to the Palestinian Authority.[65]

Madam Chairman, I should also note that you and other leaders from the House Foreign Affairs Committee issued a rather strong rebuke of the move in a letter to Mr. Kerry, as well.[66]

---

[60] Justin Jalil, "Netanyahu Derides 'Preposterous' ICC Probe of Israel," *The Times of Israel*, January 17, 2015. (http://www.timesofisrael.com/netanyahu-derided-preposterous-icc-probe-of-israel/)

[61] Allyn Fisher-Ilan, "Israel Withholds Funds, Weighs Lawsuits against Palestinians," *Reuters*, January 3, 2015. (http://www.reuters.com/article/2015/01/03/us-mideast-palestinians-israel-idUSKBN0KC07Q20150103)

[62] Ido Rosenzweig & Yuval Shany, "Establishment of a Legal Department by the Israeli Security Cabinet to Deal with Issues of International Jurisdiction," *Terrorism & Democracy*, 2009. (http://en.idi.org.il/analysis/terrorism-and-democracy/issue-no-12/establishment-of-a-legal-department-by-the-israeli-security-cabinet-to-deal-with-issues-of-international-jurisdiction/)

[63] Allyn Fisher-Ilan, "Israel Withholds Funds, Weighs Lawsuits against Palestinians," *Reuters*, January 3, 2015. (http://www.reuters.com/article/2015/01/03/us-mideast-palestinians-israel-idUSKBN0KC07Q20150103)

[64] "Obama, Netanyahu Discuss Iran Talks, Palestinian ICC Move," *Reuters*, January 12, 2015. (http://www.reuters.com/article/2015/01/13/us-usa-israel-obama-idUSKBN0KM00A20150113)

[65] Julian Pecquet, "Palestinian Authority on the Hot Seat," *Al-Monitor*, January 30, 2015. (http://www.al-monitor.com/pulse/originals/2015/01/palestinian-authority-congress-aid-icc-foreign-affairs.html)

[66] House Foreign Affairs Committee. Press Release, "House Foreign Affairs Committee Leaders Write Secretary Kerry on Palestinian Authority," January 27, 2015. (http://foreignaffairs.house.gov/press-release/house-foreign-affairs-committee-leaders-write-secretary-kerry-palestinian-authority)

Alarm in Washington over the Palestinian ICC bid is well founded, primarily because it hits close to home. The U.S. is threatened with lawfare challenges similar to those threatening Israel. Indeed, the ICC prosecutor has, since 2007, been investigating alleged crimes committed in Afghanistan, including torture and "cruel treatment" of detainees, which could target U.S. officials.[67]

In short, the campaign against Israel has wider ramifications. The United States and its allies are all vulnerable to lawfare. Lawmakers must ensure that the Palestinian bid at the ICC fails.

RECOMMENDATIONS

Madam Chairman, while I support economic measures against the Palestinian leadership for its reckless behavior, threats to cut assistance have not had the desired impact in recent years. The reason for this is simple: Washington is dependent on the Palestinian Authority for continued security cooperation with Israel. Abbas knows this. This is why he feels comfortable testing the patience of legislators, and even the president. I suggest the following steps as a means to reassert American leverage, protect American interests, empower new moderate Palestinian leadership, and safeguard Israeli security concerns.

1. **Adopt a more systematic approach to lawfare.** As my FDD colleague Orde Kittrie notes, the U.S. government's approach to lawfare has thus far been piecemeal and insufficiently proactive. Congress should strongly consider establishing a lawfare office similar to that established by Israel. Such an office could enhance the efficacy of the U.S. government's lawfare-related activities in defense of both U.S. officials and those of our close allies.

2. **Leverage America's "Article 98" agreements with foreign governments.** Countries that enter into these agreements with the U.S. agree not to surrender U.S. persons to the jurisdiction of the ICC. The U.S. has concluded such agreements with at least one hundred countries.[68] Congress should ensure that the U.S. enters into as many of these agreements as possible, and perhaps modify them to include its key allies, such as Israel. Congress might even consider conditioning U.S. military assistance on an assurance that the receiving countries include "Article 98" agreements for the U.S. and its allies. Knowing it would face severe difficulties getting access to accused U.S. and Israeli officials could deter the ICC from opening formal investigations, particularly when it is clear the charges are unfounded.

3. **Declassify intelligence on recent Palestinian terrorism, illicit activity, and human rights abuses.** Congress can work with the U.S. intelligence community to identify terrorism, illicit financial activity, and human rights abuses in both the West Bank and the Gaza Strip dating back to November 29, 2012, when the U.N. General Assembly recognized Palestine as a non-member Observer State. This, coupled with open source reports,[69] would provide the Israelis

---

[67] Brett D. Schaefer & Steven Groves, "U.S. Refusal to Ratify Rome Statute Vindicated by ICC Afghanistan Report," *Heritage Foundation Issue Brief*, December 11, 2014.
(http://www.heritage.org/research/reports/2014/12/us-refusal-to-ratify-rome-statute-vindicated-by-icc-afghanistan-report)
[68] "International Criminal Court – Article 98 Agreements Research Guide," *Georgetown University Law Library Website*, accessed January 30, 2015. (http://www.law.georgetown.edu/library/research/guides/article_98.cfm)
[69] Lazar Berman , "Human Rights Watchdog: Hamas, PA Tortured Hundreds in 2014." *The Times of Israel*

and the ICC with evidence of possible war crimes committed within the territories of the "State of Palestine." More importantly, it would send a message to the Palestinian leadership that they have as much to lose as anyone by pursuing this dangerous track. One recent report suggests significant human rights abuses.[70]

4. **Promote Palestinian political change.** Mahmoud Abbas is a huge part of the problem. Once considered a reformer, Abbas is now 10 years into a 5-year presidential term. He is also the head of the Fatah faction and the PLO. He has a stranglehold on Palestinian politics. Washington only holds on to him for fear of not knowing what comes next. We must now prepare the ground for new Palestinian Authority elections. But we must also push for real political change. So long as the Palestinian political system remains ossified, the Palestinians will be taken in by gimmicks like the "Palestine 194" campaign and the ICC. Only real political reform will put the Palestinians in a position to drop the theatrics and get back to the business of state-building. Notably, former Palestinian Prime Minister Salam Fayyad understood this, and consequently opposed the "Palestine 194" campaign.

5. **Strengthen the PA and weaken the PLO.** In the past, we have punished the PA for unilateral Palestinian maneuvers. But it is actually the PLO that is pursuing Israel at the ICC, and it is the PLO that is waging the Palestine 194 campaign. Moreover, the PLO still has terrorist groups under its umbrella.[71] Rooted in a terrorist past, its leaders are unelected, its decision-making is opaque, and its finances are obscured from the public eye. Its very existence enables a dysfunctional system. At any given time, we don't know whether it is the PLO, the Fatah faction, or the PA that is speaking in the Palestinians' name. If the goal is to hold the Palestinian leadership responsible for its actions, it is time to empower the Palestinian government we seek to engage, and to make the PLO obsolete. To that end, we must shut down the PLO embassy in Washington, and to take steps to weaken the organization worldwide.

6. **Reform Gaza.** We cannot only focus on the West Bank political structures. The Hamas-Fatah split remains a challenge that will encumber both regional peace and Palestinian reform. Hamas must be removed from the Gaza Strip if meaningful change is to take root. Washington can help bring about Hamas's demise by working with the Israelis, Egyptians, and the PA to actively undermine the terrorist group in Gaza—financially, politically and militarily.

7. **Reassert Washington's role as arbiter of the peace process.** I don't believe that peace between the current leaders is likely. Nor do I believe that this administration has earned the trust of either side. However, the next set of leaders may well make progress. But even if deadlock persists, Washington cannot abdicate its role as the honest broker. Once we return to that role, we may have an opportunity to call for a halt to all unilateral activity and guide this conflict toward a more constructive dynamic.

January 29, 2015. (http://www.timesofisrael.com/human-rights-watchdog-hamas-pa-tortured-hundreds-in-2014/)
[70] Khaled Abu Toameh. "Hamas, Palestinian Authority Step Up Human Rights Violations," *Gatestone Institute*, January 9, 2015. (http://www.gatestoneinstitute.org/5019/hamas-palestinian-authority-human-rights)
[71] Kenneth Katzman, "The PLO and its Factions," *Congressional Research Service*, June 10, 2002. (http://www.iwar.org.uk/news-archive/crs/11562.pdf)

On behalf of the Foundation for Defense of Democracies, thank you for the opportunity to testify today. I look forward to answering your questions.

Ms. Ros-Lehtinen. Professor, you are recognized. Thank you.

STATEMENT OF MR. EUGENE KONTOROVICH, PROFESSOR OF LAW, NORTHWESTERN UNIVERSITY SCHOOL OF LAW

Mr. Kontorovich. Madam Chairwoman, Ranking Member Deutch, honorable members of the committee, thank you for inviting me to testify. In my testimony today, I am going to focus on three issues: Why the Palestinian Authority's effort to join the International Criminal Court is dangerous, not just for Israel but equally for the United States; why the Court is likely to be biased toward Israel; and, finally, remedial options under United States law.

The Palestinian campaign in the ICC threatens not just Israel but U.S. diplomatic and security interests as well. Crucially, America like Israel, is not a member state of the International Criminal Court and has chosen to not subject itself to the court's jurisdiction. Thus America and Israel find themselves in the same boat in terms of wanting to avoid precedents that would allow other entities to forcibly subject them to ICC process.

There are five dangerous precedents that this could set. First of all, the Palestinians are seeking to establish a precedent where a majority vote of the General Assembly is all it takes to secure jurisdiction over a non-member state. That is an extremely dangerous precedent for the United States. The United States in creating the United Nations chose not to give any binding powers to the General Assembly, but rather to screen all of those through the Security Council. The notion that a simple majority vote of the General Assembly could create jurisdiction over the U.S. servicemen is a very dangerous one. One could imagine Boko Haram or ISIS petitioning the General Assembly and, on a good day, getting a majority vote to exercise jurisdiction over U.S. troops.

All of the particular legal issues that the Palestinians are seeking to establish and need to win on at the ICC are ones that would be very dangerous for the United States. I would like to remind the subcommittee that the United States is currently subject to a preliminary investigation about the role of U.S. troops in the treatment of detainees in Afghanistan. It has been thought there are some major principles that insulate Western democracies like the United States, the notions of complementarity and gravity.

Complementarity means that if a country conducts its own investigations or has a well-functioning legal system that investigates its troops, it does not have to worry about the ICC stepping in. Now the question is what level of abstraction you apply complementarity on. So while the United States is a well-functioning democracy, if it chooses not to investigate every particular incident, if it chooses not to investigate the roles of senior civilian leaders in alleged incidents, and the ICC chooses to step in, this would be something the United States would be very uncomfortable with. Yet nonetheless, that is exactly what the Palestinians are trying to establish vis-à-vis Israel. Israel also has a well-functioning criminal justice system. If the ICC is to take any steps forward, it would require defining complementarity at such a low level that the United States also would not be insulated by this principle.

Then there is the principle of gravity, that the ICC is reserved for the worst of the worst international crimes, mass atrocities, which its charter refers to. As a result, isolated or lower level crimes, the ICC can't deal with because in a world of millions killed in conflicts around the world, obviously the ICC can't deal with everything and needs to prioritize. The United States and other Western democracies have been shielded by this principle. This would be a principle that prevents an ICC investigation of alleged abuses in Afghanistan.

Ms. ROS-LEHTINEN. If the gentleman would suspend, I am going to kindly remind the audience for one last time, that if you cause a disruption, you will be removed from the hearing room. So when each witness finishes his or her statement, if you would remain quiet and let the order take place. If not, the Capitol Police are here, and you will be escorted out.

Please continue.

Mr. KONTOROVICH. The Palestinians at the ICC wish to establish a precedent that the mere building and buying of homes in eastern Jerusalem is a mass atrocity. If gravity is defined at such a level, any actions by U.S. forces would certainly meet that standard, and all of the limiting principles of ICC jurisdiction that had been promised to Western states as things that would insulate them would be defined essentially out of the ICC charter.

Finally, I need to mention the Monetary Gold principle. The monetary gold principle is a principle of international law that an International Court cannot decide the rights or privileges or duties of a country that has not accepted jurisdiction. The Palestinians are seeking to essentially draw Israel's borders through the International Court. Even the International Court of Justice, which is actually in the business of border disputes, can only do so with the consent of all the involved countries. The precedent that an International Court can decide on national borders and any other issue without the consent of the countries involved would threaten the United States extraordinarily, especially as a country that has opted out of the jurisdiction of the International Criminal Court.

Naturally, this would also hurt American diplomacy, as the Palestinian effort violates key provisions of the Oslo Accords and represents a wholesale repudiation of the principles not just of the Oslo Accords but also the Bush Letter, which was endorsed by Congress, not to mention Security Council Resolution 242, the League of Nations Mandate, and pretty much every diplomatic instrument in the conflict, which all call for negotiations and negotiated border resolutions.

Why is the ICC likely to be biased against Israel? Well, because the prosecutor has effectively abrogated her independence and become a spokesperson of the General Assembly. The prosecutor's recent decisions about Gaza being occupied territory and Palestine being a state, which also happened to be mutually contradictory, were adopted by simply repeating United Nations' resolutions, thus becoming an organ of a political body.

Ms. ROS-LEHTINEN. Thank you very much, Professor.

[The prepared statement of Mr. Kontorovich follows:]

The Palestinian ICC Bid and U.S. Interests

Prepared written congressional testimony of:

Eugene Kontorovich
Professor, Northwestern University School of Law

Hearing before the
House Committee on Foreign Affairs
Subcommittee on the Middle East & North Africa Hearing:

*"The Palestinian Authority's International Criminal Court
Gambit: A True Partner for Peace?"*

Washington, D.C.
February 4, 2015

Chairwoman Ros-Lehtinen, Ranking Member Deutch, and honorable members of the Subcommittee, thank you for the opportunity to discuss the Palestinian Authority's (PA) effort to use the International Criminal Court (ICC) against Israel. I am a professor of international and constitutional law at Northwestern University. One of my areas of focus is international criminal law, and I have written extensively in peer-reviewed and other law journals in the U.S. and abroad about the International Criminal Court, and possible Palestinian efforts to join it.

The Palestinian ICC campaign threatens not just Israel, but the U.S. diplomatic and security interests as well. Like Israel, the U.S. has chosen not to join the ICC, and thus has the same interest as Israel in avoiding being subject to its jurisdiction. The Palestinian bid could set dangerous precedents in this regard. The notion that ICC jurisdiction over US troops could be conferred by a majority vote of the GA should be alarming. Similarly, to pursue an investigation of Israel, the Court would have to define down important limitations on its jurisdiction. Such decisions would set precedents that could then be used aggressively against US troops and officials, who are already the subject of an examination by the Prosecutor.[1]

On the diplomatic front, the Palestinian Authority's ICC bid represents a rejection and termination of negotiations with Israel as the exclusive method of determining all "final status" issues. That repudiates what has been for decades central pillar of U.S. diplomacy with regards to the conflict. Moreover, it represents a violation of two provisions of the Oslo Accords: not to seek a final determination of the status of disputed territory outside of negotiations,[2] and exclusive Israeli jurisdiction over its nationals in the West Bank.[3] The Palestinians are asking to have both their statehood and borders declared by the ICC, without Palestinian compromise or Israeli consent, and to give to the Court a jurisdiction over Israeli civilians that the PA does not possess. As the guarantor of the Oslo Accords, the U.S.'s diplomatic credibility with its allies, and in the ME Peace Process, depends on responding to this breach.

The rest of this testimony will examine the dangerous precedents the ICC proceedings could set for the U.S. The testimony will then show why there is a considerable risk such

---

[1] ICC Office of the Prosecutor, Report on Preliminary Examinations Activities, pg. 22, http://www.icc-cpi.int/iccdocs/otp/OTP-Pre-Exam-2014.pdf (describing inquiry into the activities of U.S. forces in Afghanistan).

[2] Alan Baker, *International Criminal Court Opens Inquiry into Possible War Crimes in Palestinian Territories: A Response to UN Secretary General Ban Ki-moon from Amb. Alan Baker*, JERUSALEM CENTER FOR PUBLIC AFFAIRS (Jan. 21, 2015), http://jcpa.org/article/international-criminal-court-opens-inquiry-possible-war-crimes-palestinian-territories/.

[3] *See generally*, G.R. Watson, THE OSLO ACCORDS: INTERNATIONAL LAW AND THE ISRAELI-PALESTINIAN PEACE AGREEMENTS (Oxford University Press, 2000). While the Oslo Accords were signed with the Palestine Liberation Organization, the PA has always conducted itself, and been treated by, the international community as a party to the agreement. The PA officially changed its name to the State of Palestine after the UN vote, but continues to assert its rights under Oslo.

disregard will materialize – the ICC's built-in and demonstrated bias against Israel; and finally consider remedial options available under existing U.S. law, which are surprisingly powerful, and could even authorize a cut-off of funds to the United Nations.

Dangerous Precedents For The U.S.

While much of the discussion of the Palestinian bid has focused on its negative consequences for Israel and the peace process, the legal dangers to the United States are also considerable. The United States, like Israel, is not a member of the ICC. In deciding not to join the Rome Statute, non-members sought to limit their exposure to ICC jurisdiction. For the ICC to act against Israeli nationals, it would have to establish a number of novel precedents and rulings, which could then serve as precedents for proceedings against the U.S. Thus, in a real sense, Israelis is a proxy for the U.S. in this legal battle.

1. Empowering the General Assembly

The PA has sought ICC jurisdiction over Israel through the expedient of having the U.N. General Assembly pass a resolution referring to it as a state.[4] The Prosecutor, at least, seems willing to allow the GA to expand the Court's jurisdiction to territories that would otherwise not qualify as states under principles of international law. This exposes all non-members to a broad and indefinite danger of falling within ICC jurisdiction. In effect, the Prosecutor's view is that ICC jurisdiction over non-member states could be conferred by a vote of the General Assembly. This is both surprising and dangerous, as the GA otherwise lacks any substantive powers. Given its composition and voting patterns, the U.S. and other great powers would certainly not entrust the General Assembly with such a role. Moreover, the Prosecutor's view contradicts the clear policy of the Rome Statute, where the only U.N. body with control over the Court's jurisdiction is the Security Council.[5] This suggests that at most, only Security Council decisions about U.N. membership can conclusively determine "statehood" for ICC purposes.

Now, in the Prosecutor's view, all an entity needs to do to be able to invoke the ICC's jurisdiction is win a bare majority vote of the General Assembly. It need not control territory or satisfy any of the objective criteria of statehood. In this view, the Islamic State, the Taliban, or Boko Haram are all but one G.A. vote away from joining the ICC and seeking investigations of the U.S and its allies. While this may seem far-fetched, Palestinian ICC membership was also seen as unlikely even a decade ago.

A more immediate threat of this type for the U.S. would include Cuba joining the ICC,

---

[4] U.N. Doc. A/RES/67/19 (Nov. 29, 2012) *available at*, http://www.un.org/en/ga/search/view_doc.asp?symbol=A/RES/67/19.

[5] *See* Rome Statute Art. 13(b)& 16, *available at* http://www.icc-cpi.int/nr/rdonlyres/ea9aeff7-5752-4f84-be94-0a655eb30e16/0/rome_statute_english.pdf (providing that the Council can both refer investigations and suspend investigations). Crucially, only situations referred by the Council need not occur in the territory of sovereign states. Art. 12(b).

and referring alleged U.S. crimes in Guantanamo Bay.[6] Whether the naval base is in the "territory" of Cuba for ICC purposes seems ambiguous, as it has never exercised any sovereignty there since the creation of the Court. However, the Palestinian precedent would favor jurisdiction, as it shows no actual exercise of sovereignty is required.

2. *Complementarity*

The two primary jurisdictional barriers to an ICC investigation are defined in Art. 17 of the Rome Statute: complementarity (the existence of good faith national investigations or prosecutions) and gravity (the crimes must be of a particularly serious nature, even given that most of the crimes within the Court's jurisdiction are inherently grave). Complementarity was thought to be a major safeguard against ICC investigations into Western democracies with well-functioning legal systems. Such countries have "nothing to fear"[7] from the ICC, jurists have often assured, because presumably they deal reasonably with their own crimes.[8]

Israel, certainly, is a robust and open democracy with a well-functioning military justice system. It investigates and prosecutes violations of the laws of war by its armed forces. Thus any ICC investigation over alleged crimes committed by Israel in Gaza would, if it proceeds, have to find this level of "complementarity" insufficient, perhaps on the theory that merely focusing on direct perpetrators and not the chain of command is insufficient. This theory would also make it difficult for the U.S. to assert complementarity.

One of the primary goals of the Palestinian effort is an investigation of Israeli civilian communities in the West Bank ("settlements"). This also threatens to define complementarity in a way dangerous to the U.S. While Israel has a proven track record of investigating war crimes by its forces, after open and serious consideration of the question, it does not regard the existence of these civilian communities to amount to the "deportation or transfer" of civilians into occupied territory in contravention of Art. 49(6) of the Geneva Conventions. Such a view is at least reasonable, because there is simply no contrary precedent, as there have never been any prosecutions for this offense.

If such good faith views of substantive law do not satisfy complementarity, the implications go far beyond Israel. Many Western democracies have policies or programs that, in their view, are consistent with international law, even when this view is widely contested. For example, the U.S. is not prosecuting or investigating anyone for drone strikes against terror groups abroad because it is of the good faith opinion that the program is legal. Yet this view is not widely shared in international law circles. If complementarity does not insulate a country's honest and independent judgment about

---

[6] A prominent scholar of the Court has explicitly supported such jurisdiction. *See* WILLIAM SCHABAS, THE INTERNATIONAL CRIMINAL COURT: A COMMENTARY ON THE ROME STATUTE 285 (2010).

[7] *International Criminal Court Bill [Lords]*, WWW.PARLIMENT.UK, http://www.publications.parliament.uk/pa/cm200001/cmstand/d/st010501/am/10501s02.htm (last visited Feb. 1, 2015).

[8] *See e.g., Id* (remarks of Solicitor-General of the United Kingdom).

the requirements of international law, it will also not protect the U.S. in any case where its interpretations do not command the Prosecutor's assent.[9]

3. Gravity.[10]

The ICC's mission is to deal with the world's worst crimes – with "atrocities that deeply shock the conscience of humanity," in the words of the Rome Statute's preamble. This focus on mass atrocities is ensured through the gravity requirement. While the crimes within the Court's jurisdiction are all serious, it can only deal with those situations where they are committed with particular "gravity" – that is, the worst of the worst.[11] The gravity requirement has been particularly important in limiting the ICC's jurisdiction over nationals of Western democracies. For example, the Prosecutor did not proceed with a war crimes investigation of British soldiers over alleged unlawful killings in Iraq because the number of victims – under 20 – failed to meet the gravity test.[12] The gravity test is particularly relevant to the U.S. given the Prosecutor's ongoing preliminary investigation into alleged U.S. abuse of detainees. In the account in the Senate's recent report, such alleged victims number in the dozens. This would surely fail the gravity test, unless the bar is lowered to squeeze in Israel.

It remains unclear precisely how to measure the "gravity" of a situation or crime. In practice, the prosecutor looks primarily at the number of victims and the nature of the crimes. Genocide and crimes against humanity top the list; among war crimes, those involving killing, sexual violence and other forms of physical brutality are the gravest. Again, even the killing of innocent civilians has been found not to satisfy gravity when the number of victims is too small.[13]

An investigation of Israeli settlements would set the gravity bar so low, anything else would qualify. It would effectively eliminate gravity as a limit on jurisdiction, letting the court mix mass atrocities with minor infractions. For the act of "transferring" civilians into occupied territory does not involve any killing or physical abuse. Indeed it lacks victims in the classic sense. It is a classic victimless crime: at least in the conventional

---

[9]The question is whether the ICC would pay the same deference to good faith national determinations of disputable questions of international law as federal courts must pay to state court determinations of constitutional law in *habeas corpus* cases. See, e.g., Williams v. Taylor, 529 U.S. 362 (2000); Teague v. Lane, 489 U.S. 288 (1989). The rule the Palestinians hope to apply to Israel would effectively give the ICC power to ignore reasonable good faith national interpretations of international law when it happens to disagree with those interpretations.

[10] The discussion here is based on Eugene Kontorovich, *When Gravity Fails: Israeli Settlements and Admissibility in the International Criminal Court*, 47 ISRAEL LAW REVIEW 379-99 (2014).

[11]*See* Rome Statute Art. 17, *available at* http://www.icc-cpi.int/nr/rdonlyres/ea9aeff7-5752-4f84-be94-0a655eb30e16/0/rome_statute_english.pdf

[12]*See* Prosecutor's Letter In Response To Allegations Of War Crimes Committed During the Invasion of Iraq, INTERNATIONAL CRIMINAL COURT: OFFICE OF THE PROSECUTOR (Feb. 9, 2006) *available at*, http://www.icc-cpi.int/NR/rdonlyres/04D143C8-19FB-466C-AB77-4CDB2FDEBEF7/143682/OTP_letter_to_senders_re_Iraq_9_February_2006.pdf. .

[13]*Id.*

account, even consensual property transactions between Jews and Arabs constitute illegal settlements. Indeed, the reason NGOs fly over Israeli settlements photographing new construction is because the nominal victims, the Palestinians, might not otherwise even know of the alleged injurious act of house building.

The lack of gravity is underscored by the Prosecutor's failure to investigate such conduct in other areas, despite clearly having jurisdiction. Turkey has a massive settlement enterprise in occupied northern Cyprus. The Republic of Cyprus has been a member of the Court since its inception, and in 2014, a group of Cypriot refugees and a member of the European parliament filed a formal complaint to the ICC.[14] Yet the prosecutor has taken no action, despite having clear jurisdiction back to 2002. Similarly, the Prosecutor excluded any settlement related issues from the investigation of Russian crimes in Georgia, despite an open settlement program in Abkhazia.[15]

The failure of the ICC – and indeed any tribunal anywhere – to act against "settlements" where it has jurisdiction underscores their relative lack of gravity. If anything, the Cypriot situation presents a much stronger case for gravity, as the majority of the population in the occupied territory are now settlers, thus implicating the prohibition's core policies of preventing fundamental demographic change.[16] The widespread notion that the Prosecutor may nonetheless open an investigation into Israel's actions only underscores the general expectation that the ICC will fail to act in accordance with its general practice and established law.

Yet, if allowing private citizens to buy or build houses in eastern Jerusalem 1000 yards across the Green Line were one of the "gravest" crimes, it would be very hard to maintain that the torture of even a few detainees would not also meet the test. Indeed, many advocates of the ICC have never been fond of the gravity requirement, seeing it – correctly – as a limit on the powers of the institution. International law scholars like William Schabas have long called for interpreting the requirement very narrowly, and the Palestinian initiative may be seen as the perfect occasion.

---

[14]*MEP Costas Mavrides & Cypriots Against Turkish War Crimes (The Complainants) v. The Republic of Turkey (Accused of War Crimes)*, INTERNATIONAL CRIMINAL COURT: COMMUNICATION TO THE PROSECUTOR OF THE INTERNATIONAL CRIMINAL COURT REGARDING THE SITUATION IN OCCUPIED CYPRUS (July 14, 2014), *available at*
https://dl.dropboxusercontent.com/u/92018228/Communication%20-%20ICC%20Turkey.pdf.

[15] Eugene Kontorovich, *ICC Prosecutor Says Full Inquiry into Russian War Crimes Might Come Soon, But Omits Some Crimes* (Dec. 10, 2014), http://www.ejiltalk.org/icc-prosecutor-says-full-inquiry-into-russian-war-crimes-might-come-soon-but-omits-some-crimes/.

[16] Ahmet Atasoy, *Population Geography Of The Turkish Republic Of Northern Cyprus*, MUSTAFA KEMAL UNIVERSITY JOURNAL OF SOCIAL SCIENCES INSTITUTE 16(8): 29-62, at 38 (2011); Ambassador Ronald Schlicher, *Turkish Cypriot Census Debate Focuses On Natives Versus "Settlers"*, May 18, 2007, *available at* http://www.wikileaks.org/plusd/cables/07NICOSIA434_a.html.

4. Monetary Gold *Principle and the rights of non-members*[17]

The Palestinian effort at the ICC is not about seeking "justice," but about having an international institution anoint them as a state and fully endorse their negotiating positions about borders – without any negotiation or concession on the Palestinian part. From that position, they could then expand their negotiating demands. Thus the core of the effort is securing ICC jurisdiction over Israeli settlements, which would require the Court to determine that all of the West Bank is already Palestinian territory.

Even if there were currently Palestinian state, it is clear that its borders remain undetermined, and that the areas of the settlements in particular are excluded from them. Indeed, this is why international organizations and countries call for negotiations to establish borders – because they do not currently exist. The common denominator of all international pronouncements on the issue is that the border, when established, will not be the 1949 Armistice Lines. Indeed, under current agreements Israel maintains jurisdiction over these areas, and thus they cannot be presumed to be Palestinian, even assuming there was a Palestinian state.[18]

But regardless of where the border will be, should be, or is, the ICC is powerless to determine the borders of "Palestine." That is because doing so would also determine the borders and legal rights of Israel. Under a well-established principle of international law (known as the *Monetary Gold* rule, after the International Court of Justice case where it was announced) an international court cannot adjudicate a matter that affects the rights of a third country if that country does not accept its jurisdiction.[19] Thus the court that does decide many border controversies in the international system – the ICJ – does so only when all sides agree to submit a dispute to it. Indeed, the ICC was never given the power to determine the rights of states, but rather only to determine individual criminal responsibility.

The current Palestinian effort seeks to give the ICC massive unilateral powers even beyond those of the ICJ (much as it also depends on creating new powers for the General Assembly). Such a role for the ICC was never contemplated. If the Court thinks it can ignore the fundamental *Monetary Gold* rule, it poses a threat to all non-member states (and even to members who joined on the understanding that the court would only determine the guilt of individuals, not the borders of sovereigns).

---

[17] The discussion here is based on Eugene Kontorovich, *Israel/Palestine – The ICC's Uncharted "Territory,"* 11 JOURNAL OF INTERNATIONAL CRIMINAL JUSTICE 979-99 (2013).

[18] *See* The Israeli-Palestinian Interim Agreement On The West Bank And The Gaza Trip, Annex IV – Protocol Concerning Legal Affairs, Art. I § 2 (Sept. 28, 1995), *available at* http://www.mfa.gov.il/MFA/ForeignPolicy/Peace/Guide/Pages/THE%20ISRAELI-PALESTINIAN%20INTERIM%20AGREEMENT%20-%20Annex%20IV.aspx#article1.

[19] *Italy v. France, United Kingdom of Great Britain and Northern Ireland and United States of America,* INTERNATIONAL COURT OF JUSTICE (June 15, 1954) *available at,* http://www.icj-cij.org/docket/index.php?sum=279&p1=3&p2=3&case=19&p3=5 (Monetary Gold Removed From Rome in 1943).

Can The ICC be A Fair Tribunal?

<u>Bias built into the Rome Statute</u>

The Court's foundational statute[20] (the Rome Statute) contains a provision specifically designed to target Israel.[21] The history bears reviewing. The elaborate definition of war crimes in the Rome Statute (Art. 8) is borrowed largely from the Geneva Conventions and other related treaties.[22] Yet at the 1999 drafting conference, a group of Arab states secured one significant change in the Rome Statute provision corresponding to IV Geneva Art. 49(6), prohibiting an occupying power from "deporting or transferring" its civilian population into the occupied territory. This was an odd provision to tinker with, since it had seen no prosecutions in any international or national courts in its history.

Yet the Arab states prevailed at negotiations to have the ICC provision prohibit "directly *or indirectly* deporting or transferring"[23] (they had originally asked for even broader language).[24] In law the difference between direct and indirect effects is quite significant. The Rome Statute language has no parallel or precedent in international law, and was generally understood as seeking to go beyond what is prohibited by Geneva Conventions to encompass the self-motivated migration of Israelis into the West Bank (and back then, Gaza). It was designed to make "facilitation" a crime – i.e., to turn the negative prohibition on "transfer" into a newfangled positive obligation on a government to discourage or prevent its nationals from migrating into a territory under its control, discriminating on the basis of nationality or ethnicity. The novelty of the provision is evident from the observation that the U.S. would have been guilty of violating it during its 45-year occupation of West Berlin, when it enabled and even encouraged Americans to move to the city.

Thus the Rome Statute from the start was uniquely written to target Israel, the only nation to be thus honored. The notion that the provision is understood to target Israel is further supported by the experience of Cyprus, an original state party to the Rome Statute. Despite Cypriot efforts to petition the prosecutor, no one thinks there is a real chance that Turkey might have to answer for its massive settlement enterprise in the occupied north

---

[20] Rome Statute, *available at* http://www.icc-cpi.int/nr/rdonlyres/ea9aeff7-5752-4f84-be94-0a655eb30e16/0/rome_statute_english.pdf.

[21] See Art. Article 8(2)(b)(viii):

[22] *See War crimes under the Rome Statute of the International Criminal Court and their source in international humanitarian law   Table*, INTERNATIONAL COMMITTEE OF THE RED CROSS (Oct. 31, 2012), *available at*, https://www.icrc.org/en/document/war-crimes-under-rome-statute-international-criminal-court-and-their-source-international#.VM8BmGTF_Iw.

[23] ROY S.K. LEE, THE INTERNATIONAL CRIMINAL COURT: THE MAKING OF THE ROME STATUTE : ISSUES, NEGOTIATIONS AND RESULTS 112-13 (1999).

[24] Proposal submitted by Algeria et al. on article 8(2)(b)(viii): War crime of deporting or transferring population, PREPARATORY COMMISSION FOR THE INTERNATIONAL CRIMINAL COURT: WORKING GROUP ON ELEMENTS OF CRIMES, PCNICC/1999/WGEC/DP.25 (Aug. 10, 1999) *available at*, http://www.legal-tools.org/uploads/tx_ltpdb/doc16864.pdf.

of the island.[25] Observers implicitly understand that the "directly or indirectly" provision is a legal bullet with Israel's name on it. Yet if the Court were to investigate Israeli settlements, despite multiple jurisdictional barriers, while ignoring Turkish ones, where there is a 12-year backlog of jurisdiction, it would deprive the proceedings of any legitimacy.

Moreover, that a group of Arab states (including, ironically, Morocco,[26] author of perhaps the most ambitious settler enterprise in Western Sahara, which the Palestinians happen to support) expanded the provision shows that they understood that the Geneva language fits at best imperfectly with the diverse patterns of Jewish migration into the West Bank (which include both government-supported building projects and private construction and purchase, property belonging to Jews from before 1949, outposts built in defiance of government regulations, and so forth).To be sure, the Court might ultimately interpret the Rome Statute provision to be entirely congruent with the Geneva one, which itself has never been interpreted. But Israel quite reasonably does not want to be the test subject for interpreting new rule designed solely for it.

The Geneva provision, incidentally, was designed to protect against fundamental demographic changes in the occupied territory (what the Nuremberg prosecutions called "obliterate[ing] the former national character of these territories.") The re-write of it for the ICC is unfaithful to those policies, as it is rather hard to purposefully effect fundamental demographic change through mere indirection or facilitation, as the example of Israel proves. The Israeli settlements have not come close to effecting such a change; after nearly five decades, the settler population remains a small fraction (less than 10%) of the total population of the territories the Palestinians claim are occupied. Indeed, Palestinian claims of demographic ascendancy not just in the territories, but also between the river and the sea, belie the notion of fundamental demographic change. In occupied Cyprus, by contrast, settlers have reached a major demographic tipping point, constituting roughly half the population. If the Court were interested in setting precedent on settlements, this would be a logical place to start.

Bias from weakness

Now we'll turn to the Court as an institution. In the wake of the Palestinian turn to the International Criminal Court, several commentators have argued that there is no reason to think the institution is out to get Israel. That is true, simply because the Court has done so little in its twelve-year history, that it is hard to say anything with confidence about its inclinations and proclivities. Prosecutions of Israelis (nationals of a non-member state)

---

[25] Eugene Kontorovich, *Cyprus & the ICC – international reactions*, THE VOLOKH CONSPIRACY (Aug. 8, 2014), http://www.washingtonpost.com/news/volokh-conspiracy/wp/2014/08/08/cyprus-the-icc-international-reactions/.

[26] Eugene Kontorovich, *The EU is right about Western Sahara – which means it is wrong about Israel*, GLOBALPOST (Nov. 21, 2013, 1:16 AM), http://www.globalpost.com/dispatches/globalpost-blogs/commentary/eu-holds-contradictory-view-settlements-west-bank-and-western.

would be a kind of activity the Court has never engaged in without the request of the Security Council, so there is even less data.

Yet there is reason to think that the Court is a most improper venue for sorting the Israeli-Palestinian conflict. Indeed, even absent any bias, the Court is structured in a way that cannot do equal justice, and is thus properly seen as a Palestinian tool against Israel. Moreover, recent statements by the Prosecutor give troubling evidence that she may be willing to replace legal analysis with the off-the-shelf political views of the "international community" on the conflict.

It is important to understand why, despite their systematic war crimes, the Palestinians see the ICC jurisdiction as a good gamble. Many distinguished jurists and academics not unsympathetic to the Palestinians have warned them that they have more to lose than gain from ICC proceedings. But they went ahead anyway, which means they have a different analysis – one that it is useful to understand.

The Court's track record suggests it is incapable of rendering impartial justice in an ongoing bilateral conflict. The Court is not some well-established, Olympian seat of judgment. Rather, it is a weak, conflicted and floundering institution, beset by profound embarrassments that might affect its decision-making.[27] In 12 years, it has completed only three cases, with two convictions. Most recently, it has seen two of its highest-profile matters – the only ones involving sitting heads of state – disintegrate. These were the prosecutions of Kenya's president for election violence, and of Sudan's president, Bashir, for genocide. Both proceedings failed because of the persistent non-cooperation of the target regime. (Despite their current embrace of the ICC, the Palestinians have long been on record opposing the ICC's arrests warrant against Sudan's President Bashir.) The ICC has proven itself completely incapable of prosecuting a case against an unwilling regime, especially an authoritarian or illiberal one willing to intimidate witnesses and destroy evidence.

This is in part why the Palestinians have turned to the ICC, despite warnings from even some of their sympathizers that they will be subject to multiple possible prosecutions for war crimes. The Kenyatta case has created a playbook for countries wanting to frustrate ICC proceedings,[28] especially if they have little to fear in the way of sanctions. Quite simply, nothing suggests that the Palestinians have had a Damascene moment and decided to open themselves up to international justice and accountability. Rather, they have calculated that they can nominally accept legal exposure while maintaining de facto impunity. Noncooperation with ICC investigations is easy in a place like Gaza, where the

---

[27] Eugene Kontorovich, *A Court's Collapse: The International Criminal Court gives up on its prosecution of Kenyan president Uhuru Kenyatta*, NATIONAL REVIEW ONLINE (Sept. 15, 2014, 4:00 AM), http://www.nationalreview.com/article/387935/courts-collapse-eugene-kontorovich.

[28] Tristan McConnell, *How Kenya took on the International Criminal Court*, GLOBALPOST (Mar. 25, 2014, 5:58 PM), http://www.globalpost.com/dispatch/news/regions/africa/kenya/140325/how-kenya-beat-the-international-criminal-court.

killing of "collaborators" is institutionalized. No one will say to ICC officials, "look, there was a Hamas launcher in this school here."

Nor will the Palestinians be punished for non-cooperation – just as Kenya and Sudan have not been. Indeed, it is likely that the Palestinians will claim that as a "state under occupation" they simply cannot cooperate with investigators on-the-ground since they will claim they are (for these purposes) completely under Israel's thumb. In Israel, on the other hand, a bevy of Israeli NGOs will be lined up to supply the prosecutor with the dirt on alleged Israeli misdeeds, and many jurisdictions are only looking for an occasion to impose sanctions on Israel.

In short, unless one ascribes to the Palestinian leadership a heroic level of altruism, their accepting the Court's jurisdiction despite their well-documented war crimes suggests they anticipate the Court to be structurally biased towards them.

Bias from the General Assembly

Some have argued that, despite the rampant bias against Israel in United Nations organizations, there is no reason to suspect partiality from the Court, composed of jurists from around the world and charged with acting apolitically.

Unfortunately, the Prosecutor has already revealed that "political" decisions (i.e., General Assembly resolutions) will not be separated from the legal, but rather will be adopted in place of legal standard. In her recent memo on the Gaza flotilla matter,[29] the Prosecutor concluded that, despite Israel's complete withdrawal, Gaza is occupied because the "international community" thinks it is. This disturbing move undermines the ICC's independence by importing the political judgments of the GA and substituting them for legal standards.

The Prosecutor ignored existing legal definitions[30] and precedents about the definition and duration of "belligerent occupation," and instead simply plugged in the conclusions of GA resolutions.[31] "Belligerent occupation" is a legal term with legal definitions. One is supplied by the International Committee of the Red Cross, whose own manual provides that:

---

[29] *Situation on Registered Vessels of Comoros, Greece Cambodia: Article 53(1) Report*, INTERNATIONAL CRIMINAL COURT: THE OFFICE OF THE PROSECUTOR (Nov. 6, 2014), *available at* http://www.icc-cpi.int/iccdocs/otp/OTP-COM-Article_53%281%29-Report-06Nov2014Eng.pdf.

[30] Eugene Kontorovich, *Why Gaza is not remotely occupied (I)*, THE VOLOKH CONSPIRACY (Nov. 13, 2014), http://www.washingtonpost.com/news/volokh-conspiracy/wp/2014/11/13/why-gaza-is-not-remotely-occupied-i/.

[31] Eugene Kontorovich, *Why Gaza is not remotely occupied (II)*, THE VOLOKH CONSPIRACY (Nov. 13, 2014), http://www.washingtonpost.com/news/volokh-conspiracy/wp/2014/11/13/gaza-is-not-remotely-occupied-ii/.

> **"Occupation ceases when the occupying forces are driven out of**
> **or evacuate the territory"**[32] (emphasis in the original).

Furthermore, the question of occupation in a territory where the "occupant" has no soldiers is not one of first impression. The International Court of Justice in 2005 ruled that Uganda's control of areas of the Democratic Republic of Congo through an allied militia does not amount to an occupation,[33] despite Uganda's significant clout there. By this standard, the control of Gaza by a *hostile* militia could not be considered an occupation. The Prosecutor never even bothered dealing with this important recent ICJ precedent.

The lazy substitution of General Assembly conclusions for actual legal standards continued and took more dramatic form when the Prosecutor accepted that Palestine is a "state" for ICC purposes. For one, the conclusion that it is a "state" directly contradicts her finding just a few months earlier that Gaza (and presumably the West Bank) has continuously been under Israeli occupation despite the complete withdrawal of Israel's presence and rule. To be occupied, a territory must be under the "control" of the occupier, who functions as the government. To become a state, a territory must be governed by its own government. One cannot become a state under a condition of occupation.

The Prosecutor attempted to gloss over this glaring contradiction by saying that she did not actually determine that Palestine qualifies as a "state" under the well-established legal definitions of the term. Rather, she said that the U.N. General Assembly's vote in 2012 to call Palestine a "non-member state" is dispositive of the question. In short, she substituted the determination of the General Assembly for her own. The GA is not a judicial body, but a rather political one. Its determinations are political, not legal. (It also has no power under the U.N. Charter, to create or recognize states.)

Statehood, however, is a legal term, with legal criteria ("the Montevideo test"), which involves judgment and the application of law to facts. Of particular relevance is the requirement that to *become* a state, a territory must have a functioning government exercising supreme control in at least part of its claimed territory. The requirements for the creation of a state do not mirror those for its extinguishing. Thus the possibility of a "state under occupation," to use the Palestinian's favored term, does not preempt the need for there to first be a state under Montevideo definitions. The Palestinians, however, claim all of their territory is and has always been under the control of Israel.

The U.N. General Assembly need not be troubled by such legal problems because it is an explicitly political body. It need not be coherent or consistent, unlike a Court. For the Prosecutor to take the judgments of such a body on the application of legal terms in the

---

[32] *The Law of Armed Conflict: Belligerent Occupation*, INTERNATIONAL COMMITTEE OF THE RED CROSS (June 2002), *available at* https://www.icrc.org/eng/assets/files/other/law9_final.pdf.

[33] *Armed Activities on the Territory of the Congo (Democratic Republic of the Congo v. Uganda)*, *Judgment, I.C.J. Reports 2005, p. 168, available at* http://www.icj-cij.org/docket/files/116/10455.pdf.

Rome Statute to particular facts as binding upon the Court is to surrender her independence. The Court's statute demands and proclaims its independence. Yet decisions like this one violate the Court's independence, making it a mere organ of the U.N., and of the General Assembly at that.

There is no basis for the Prosecutor to defer to the General Assembly in this matter.[34] Unlike with other treaties, the existence of a "state" is a jurisdictional requirement under Art. 12. The Court must independently confirm the existence of its jurisdiction, according to Art. 19 and the customary practice of international courts with regard to jurisdiction. All this shows that whatever the case may be for membership in treaties, for the jurisdiction of the Court, the General Assembly's views cannot be conclusive.[35]

Finally, the Rome Statute must trump "the practice of the Secretary General" (invoked by the Prosecutor to justify following the General Assembly). Under the Statute, any political role in determining statehood would logically fall to the Security Council rather than the General Assembly. The ICC Statute creates particular powers and duties for the Security Council, and none for the General Assembly. The Council can both initiate and suspend investigations. The Assembly, under the text of the statute, cannot do anything. Thus, the Council is an express part of the "ICC system" in a way the Assembly is not. Moreover, the Council's particular role is quite relevant — it is the only avenue available to the Court to obtain territorial jurisdiction over crimes that do not occur within a territory of a state that has accepted the Court's jurisdiction.

Thus the Security Council would be the obvious route under the ICC statute for creating jurisdiction over a situation like Palestine, where statehood is far from clear. The fact that such a route is politically unlikely is of course not a bug, but a feature. Putting such jurisdiction in the hands of the SC is done to make it difficult to exercise.

Thus the statute of Court, its structure, and the repeated actions of the Prosecutor, demonstrate a built in targeting of Israel, an inability to do justice between the parties, and a pattern of parroting the political, and notoriously anti-Israel, positions of the General Assembly.

Available Measures Under Existing Legislation

The United States' opposition to the Palestinian move is not based on any special solicitude for Israel. Rather, it is a natural consequence of the U.S. position that Palestine is not a state and thus such a move depends on the ICC violating its charter, and the

---

[34] Alan Baker, *International Criminal Court Opens Inquiry into Possible War Crimes in Palestinian Territories: A Response to UN Secretary General Ban Ki-moon from Amb. Alan Baker*, JERUSALEM CENTER FOR PUBLIC AFFAIRS (Jan. 21, 2015), http://jcpa.org/article/international-criminal-court-opens-inquiry-possible-war-crimes-palestinian-territories/.

[35] Moreover, it is far from clear the GA determined Palestine was a state, rather than that it should become one. *See id.*

Palestinians the Oslo Accords. As a non-member, the U.S. shares many common interests with Israel in establishing correct precedents here.

Thus a vigorous U.S. response is appropriate. Yet the best legislative response is not obvious. Most discussions on U.S. responses have focused on cutting funding to the Palestinian Authority. This is appropriate, but inadequate. Even if it leads to the Palestinians withdrawing from the Court, it may not stop the Court from proceeding anyway, on the theory that the jurisdiction already ostensibly given cannot be retracted. Furthermore, funding to the ICC is already restricted under current law.

This does not mean that aid to the Palestinians should not be cut – though future legislation should be structured to incentivize a Palestinian withdrawal from the Court and cancellation of their 12(3) declaration. Yet there is other, less appreciated possibilities for responses under existing U.S. law that may be more effective.

This section will explore how existing legislation affects the Palestinian bid.

Cutting off funding to the PA

The 2015 Omnibus appropriations measure bars the provision of Economic Support Funds to the Palestinian Authority if they "initiate an International Criminal Court judicially authorized investigation, or actively support such an investigation, that subjects Israeli nationals to an investigation for alleged crimes against Palestinians."[36] A "judicially authorized investigation" apparently refers to a full investigation authorized by the ICC's Pre-Trial Chamber.[37] The Prosecutor's current "preliminary examination" most likely does not qualify, especially if the word "investigation" in the statute is understood to track the use of that term in the Rome Statute. On the other hand, if the Pre-Trial Chamber does authorize an investigation – the next step in the process – the Palestinians have "initiated" it for purposes of the statute. That is because the Palestinian filing of a declaration under 12(3) of the Rome Statute begins the process leading to the investigation. A 12(3) declaration leads immediately to a preliminary examination, which is the only route to an investigation[38] (unlike merely joining the court, which does not trigger a preliminary examination). Thus "initiate" means take the first step. It cannot mean to take the last step, because the Palestinians cannot directly order an investigation. By definition, only the Court can launch a judicially authorized investigation, and thus reading the term to mean "commence" would simply not make sense. This is confirmed by the language about "supporting" an investigation. The Palestinians already have said they will provide support for an investigation by providing dossiers about alleged crimes.

---

[36] Consolidated and Further Continuing Appropriations Act of 2015, Pub. L. No. 113-235, 128 Stat. 2130.

[37] *See* Rome Statute Art. 15(3)-(4), *available at* http://www.icc-cpi.int/nr/rdonlyres/ca9acff7-5752-4f84-be94-0a655eb30e16/0/rome_statute_english.pdf.

[38] *The Prosecutor of the International Criminal Court, Fatou Bensouda, opens a preliminary examination of the situation in Palestine,* INTERNATIONAL CRIMINAL COURT (Jan. 16, 2015), http://www.icc-cpi.int/en_menus/icc/press%20and%20media/press%20releases/Pages/pr1083.aspx.

That said, with the ICC, as with many courts, the process is often the punishment. Thus allowing funding to be cut off at the late stage of a full investigation would reward the PA for its breaches of Oslo and abuse of international institutions.

Cutting off funding to the UN

Existing law may require the suspension of all funds to the United Nations. The Foreign Relations Authorization Act, Fiscal Years 1990 and 1991, Pub.L. No. 101-246, 104 Stat. 70, provides:

> "(a) Prohibition. – No funds authorized to be appropriated by this Act or any other Act shall be available for the United Nations or any specialized agency thereof which accords the Palestine Liberation Organization the same standing as member states."

This law is widely described as requiring the defunding of UN organizations that admit the Palestinians as *members*. However, the language of the law is broader than mere grants of membership – it speaks of the "same standing" as members, which is a broader category than mere membership. This can be confirmed by comparison with other laws that specifically distinguish membership and standing.[39] Thus actions that fall short of full membership can fall within the "same standing" prohibition.

Under the position taken by the ICC Prosecutor[40] and, apparently, the UN Secretary General, the General Assembly vote in 2012 to call the PA a "non-member state" automatically gives them a privilege thus far only reserved to U.N. members. Applications to join the ICC are submitted to the Secretary General of the UN, pursuant to Art. 125(3) of the ICC's Rome Statute. That same provision provides that only "States" can join. By accepting the PA's instrument of accession, the Secretary General gave them the same "standing" as member states of the UN, which can join the ICC without question. Similarly, if the Prosecutor is correct that the GA vote allows the Palestinians to join the ICC regardless of whether they are in fact a state, then they enjoy the same standing as full-fledged U.N. members for ICC purposes. (The only other UN "non-member state" is not a member of the ICC; other non-members like Kosovo are also generally considered ineligible for ICC membership.) In practice, joining the ICC without an inquiry into statehood is a privilege solely of U.N. member states.

---

[39]*See* Consolidated and Further Continuing Appropriations Act of 2015, Pub. L. No. 113-235, 128 Stat. 2130 (cuts off funding to Palestinians if they "obtain the same standing as member states or full membership as a state in the United Nations or any specialized agency thereof outside an agreement negotiated between Israel and the Palestinians"); *see also* Foreign Relations Authorization Act, Fiscal Years 1994 and 1995, Pub. L. No. 103-236, 108 Stat. 454 (cutting funding to "any affiliated organization of the United Nations which grants full membership as a state to any organization or group that does not have the internationally recognized attributes of statehood").

[40]*The Prosecutor of the International Criminal Court, Fatou Bensouda, opens a preliminary examination of the situation in Palestine*, INTERNATIONAL CRIMINAL COURT (Jan. 16, 2015), http://www.icc-cpi.int/en_menus/icc/press%20and%20media/press%20releases/Pages/pr1083.aspx.

"Standing" does not mean membership; it means the ability to be treated in a certain way and to access legal rights. In particular, in law, "standing" means the right to access courts, and is thus particularly suited to accession to the Rome Statute. Thus an action by a UN agency that puts the Palestinian Authority on the same footing as member states – that would in the absence of the action require U.N. membership with Security Council approval – gives them the "same standing" as member states. This interpretation of the statute makes sense, as it prevents UN agencies from skirting the funding restrictions by giving the Palestinians the trappings of membership without the formality. Indeed, any other interpretation would merely collapse "same standing" into "membership."

According to the Prosecutor (and the Palestinians), the GA and/or Secretary General, gave the Palestinians the same "standing" – i.e., access to benefits – that has otherwise only been available to member states. In other words, the UN did not give the Palestinians U.N. membership, but they did give them "the standing" of UN members for the purposes of ICC accession. Under the plain language of the law, this triggers the complete cutting off of funding to the United Nations in its entirety.

It is not clear from the statute what the U.N. could do at this point to remedy the situation. One might suggest that a letter from the SC to the ICC registrar, communicating that the acceptance of accession was made in error, and the situation needs further examination, might suffice.

To be clear, the law only requires cutting off aid to the United Nations if the Prosecutor is right, and the GA vote gives the Palestinians automatic access to the ICC without any need for the Secretary General or Court to determine if they are a state. Of course, the position of the U.S. is that the GA vote had no such effect.

Thus whether the provision to cut off aid to the UN has been triggered depends on whether the American position, or the Prosecutor's position, is correct. It would be useful for Congress to write to the relevant U.N. officials (the Secretary General, the President of the GA) and inquire whether they understood their action as giving the Palestinians the same standing as members for ICC accession purposes, thus requiring a termination of their funding, or whether the Prosecutor has misinterpreted matters.

American Servicemembers' Protection Act

The United States already has extremely strong laws on the books against cooperating with or funding the International Criminal Court. These laws were motivated by America's choosing not to join the ICC, but still being concerned that it would be ensnared in its jurisdiction. Those concerns, long ridiculed by the Court's supporters, seem far more real given the progress of the Palestinian move.

Most famously, the American Servicemembers' Protection Act of 2002 authorizes the President to "use all means necessary and appropriate to bring about the release" of Americans held by or for the Court. 22 U.S.C. 7427(a). This language, contemplating the use of military force to rescue arrested American officials, led to the statute's being popularly known as the "Bomb The Hague Act."

Yet the use of force is authorized not just to release Americans, but also certain "allied persons." 22 U.S.C. 7427(b)(2). The definition of allied person includes government and military personnel of both NATO allies, and certain "major non-NATO allies" of which Israel is one. *See* 22 U.S.C. 7432(c).

Thus if a country were to fulfill a potential ICC arrest warrant for Israelis, the President would automatically be empowered to affect their release by any economic, political or military actions he saw fit. This is an unlikely scenario, but so is the Act's authorization of force to release Americans from custody in The Hague. However, as a piece of existing legislation that already groups Israel with America for ICC purposes, the American Servicemembers' Protection Act, could be a useful platform for further legislation. For example, new legislation could add Israel to the Act's provisions about cutting military aid to countries that cooperate with the ICC against the U.S.

I thank you for the opportunity to share these observations.

Ms. Ros-Lehtinen. Ms. Pletka is recognized.

**STATEMENT OF MS. DANIELLE PLETKA, SENIOR VICE PRESI-
DENT, FOREIGN AND DEFENSE POLICY STUDIES, AMERICAN
ENTERPRISE INSTITUTE**

Ms. Pletka. Thank you, Madam Chairwoman. It is a pleasure to be back.

Ms. Ros-Lehtinen. A little bit closer.

Ms. Pletka. It is harder, with the high heels and the dress, sliding your way in. Okay.

Can you hear me now?

You know, I have to say just as an aside, I am always struck by people who want to come and protest about Israel, and yet when I drive by the Syrian Embassy every day, a government that has been responsible for the death of hundreds of thousands of people, nobody seems to be standing outside. It is kind of a shame.

Thank you, again, for inviting me to speak today. I am not a lawyer. So I am not going to speak to the legal issues. I do think that it is important, however, to underscore the points that everybody has addressed here today, which are U.S. laws relative to the steps that the Palestinian Authority has taken in recent months.

P.L. 113, which passed last year, 113–76, codifies restrictions on aid to the Palestinians, and the letter of the law is quite specific. It says, Limitations, none of the funds appropriated under the heading ''economic support funds'' in this act may be available for assistance to the Palestinian Authority if, after the date of enactment, the Palestinians obtain the same standing as member states or full membership as a state in the U.N. or any specialized agency thereof outside an agreement negotiated between Israel the Palestinians.

I think that has happened. The Palestinians initiate an International Criminal Court judicially authorized investigation or actively support such an investigation that subjects Israeli nationals to an investigation for alleged crimes against Palestinians.

I think it is important to look at the letter of the law as the State Department ''decides'' whether in fact the law has been violated. There is not much room for decision-making here it seems to me.

The very conditions you have laid out on the question of standing within the U.N. and member agencies, as well as claims before the ICC, have in fact, been violated. And, legally, aid to the Palestinians should be cut off.

The U.S. provides about $400 million a year, a little less in the current request, in annual economic support funds and other funds to the West Bank and Gaza. Cutting off that aid will inevitably harm some Palestinians.

But those who desire self-governance and self-determination for the Palestinian people also have to accept the notion that the Palestinian people need to live with the choices that have been made by their leaders.

There are few who believe that the ICC case or Palestinian efforts within the U.N. will bring about the creation of a Palestine state.

But don't listen to me. Let me now quote Ambassador Dennis Ross, Dave's colleague, who spoke to this very issue:

''Since 2000 there have been three serious negotiations that culminated in offers to resolve the Israeli-Palestinian conflict. In each case, a proposal on all the core issues was made to Palestinian leaders, and the answer was either no or no response. Palestinian political culture is rooted in a narrative of injustice. Compromise is portrayed as betrayal, and negotiations, which are by definition about mutual concessions, will inevitably force any Palestinian leader to challenge his people by making a politically costly decision. But going to the United Nations does no such thing. It puts pressure on Israel and requires nothing of the Palestinians.''

In short, the U.N. and the ICC aren't about solving problems. They are about an unwillingness to negotiate and compromise for a true and lasting peace.

But going to the ICC is qualitatively different than going to the U.N.—and you didn't touch on this, but I think it is really an important distinction. At the U.N., the Palestinians and their supporters can get all the nonbinding resolutions that they want at the General Assembly, but at the Security Council, they have always been stymied by the U.S. veto. The ICC, however, resembles the Security Council in its ability to provide meaningful support. But by design, neither the U.S. nor any other nation has the ability to block ICC action.

What Palestinian leaders ultimately want from the ICC is criminal indictment, not just of individual members of the IDF and Israeli Intelligence Services but, most importantly, of the national leadership of Israel. Their aim is to harass them as individuals, to delegitimize Israel by establishing as a fact that many of its top leaders have in fact, after this happens, in theory been indicted for war crimes.

Knowing the U.S. can't veto ICC indictments, they are seeking them as an illicit form of pressure against their ostensible negotiating partners.

I want to address this question of whether, in fact, this is a double-edged sword for the Palestinians. As some have suggested, maybe they should be subjected to questions before the ICC. But that is really not relevant to them, and it is important to understand that. Look no further than the ICC-indicted leader of Sudan, Omar Bashir, who is welcomed at Arab League summits and does not fear to travel in the Arab world. This demonstrates that within their region, Palestinian leaders have nothing to fear from ICC indictments. But Israel's region is the West. And, within the West, such indictments are taken seriously and will be enforced to the degree possible. This is just another example of Palestinians taking advantage of Western ideals and institutions, not to advance them but to weaken and delegitimize them within their region.

Ms. ROS-LEHTINEN. Thank you so much.

[The prepared statement of Ms. Pletka follows:]

American Enterprise Institute for Public Policy Research

Testimony of Danielle Pletka, Senior Vice President, Foreign and Defense
Policy Studies,
American Enterprise Institute

Before the

U.S. House Foreign Affairs Subcommittee on the Middle East and North
Africa on "The Palestinian Authority's International Criminal Court Gambit:
A True Partner for Peace?"

Wednesday, February 4, 2015

American Enterprise Institute for Public Policy Research

Mme. Chairman, Mr. Deutch,

Thank you for your kind invitation to speak at this important hearing. As I underscored to your staff prior to agreeing to testify today, I wish to be absolutely clear that I am neither a lawyer, nor an expert on the International Criminal Court. I will confine my remarks today to questions of U.S. policy in relation to this, only the latest in efforts by the Palestinian Authority and its supporters to internationalize and otherwise , through both warfare and lawfare, subvert a genuine negotiation between Israel and the chosen representatives of the Palestinian people toward a secure and lasting peace.

The issue at hand is straightforward. In a letter from members of this committee to Secretary of State John Kerry, you wrote that:

> *The United Nations Secretary-General Ban Ki-moon proclaimed that the Palestinians will become ICC members on April 1, despite the State Department's objections that the PA "does not qualify to join the ICC." The ICC prosecutor Fatou Bensouda has already opened a preliminary examination regarding the current situation between Israel and the PA.*

That step was taken within days of the failure of a Palestinian promoted United Nations Security Council resolution that sought to place a timeline on negotiations between Israel and the Palestinians on the creation of a Palestinian state on terms dictated by the resolution (and highly unfavorable to Israel). (The U.N. General Assembly had previously voted to declare Palestine to be an "observer state", which, as my colleague, former UN Ambassador John Bolton points out, is "a status nowhere found in the UN Charter". UNESCO admitted "Palestine" as a member that same year.

U.S. law is clear: P.L. 113-76 codifies these "Restrictions on aid to the Palestinians":

(j) West Bank and Gaza.--

    (2) Limitations.--

(A)(i) None of the funds appropriated under the heading ``Economic Support Fund'' in this Act may be made available for assistance for the Palestinian Authority, if after the date of enactment of this Act--

(I) the Palestinians obtain the same standing as member states or full membership as a state in the United Nations or any specialized agency thereof outside an agreement negotiated between Israel and the Palestinians; or

(II) the Palestinians initiate an International Criminal Court judicially authorized investigation, or actively support such an investigation, that subjects Israeli nationals to an investigation for alleged crimes against Palestinians.

(ii) The Secretary of State may waive the restriction in paragraph (A) resulting from the application of subparagraph (A)(i)(I) if the Secretary certifies to the Committees on Appropriations that to do so is in the national security interest of the United States, and submits a report to such Committees detailing how the waiver and the continuation of assistance would assist in furthering Middle East peace.

(B)(i) The President may waive the provisions of section 1003 of Public Law 100-204 if the President determines and certifies in writing to the Speaker of the House of Representatives, the President pro tempore of the Senate, and the Committees on Appropriations that the Palestinians have not, after the date of enactment of this Act, obtained in the United Nations or any specialized agency thereof the same standing as member states or full membership as a state outside an agreement negotiated between Israel and the Palestinians.

Having spent a decade at your counterpart committee on the Senate side, I have little doubt of any Secretary of State or President's ability to waive these restrictions, relying on obfuscations and technicalities. That being said, your own legislative intent must be clear to you: The very conditions you have laid out on both the question of standing within the U.N. and member agencies as well as claims before the International Criminal Court have been violated. Aid to the Palestinians should be cut off.

Allow me for a moment to preview the arguments that will be brandished against those of you who wish to uphold this law of the land:

- Cutting off aid will only hurt the Palestinian people.
- This is the only way to advance the cause of a homeland for the Palestinian people.
- This will undercut the International Criminal Court and the legitimacy of the United Nations.

The Palestinians of the West Bank and Gaza are among the recipients of the highest amounts of overseas assistance (per capita) in the world today. The United States provides approximately $400 million in annual Economic Support and other funding to the West Bank and Gaza. Interestingly, CRS reports that in addition to other programs, "[d]irect U.S. budgetary assistance to the PA goes toward paying off its commercial debt, as the following FY2013 USAID congressional notification language says: Direct budget support will be used in the same manner as previous transfers—to service debt to commercial suppliers and commercial banks.

Debt to commercial banks will be debt originally incurred for purchases from commercial suppliers."

Let me translate that for you: U.S. taxpayer funded aid to the Palestinians is paying commercial sellers and banks for debts incurred by the PA. Both George W. Bush and Barack Obama have issued waivers to U.S. law to allow these transfers to the Palestinian Authority to take place.

Cutting off aid will indeed inevitably harm some Palestinians, I have little doubt. Unfortunately, this is the price of independence. Those who desire self-governance and self-determination for the Palestinian people must also accept that the Palestinian people must live with the choices made by their elected leaders.

There are few who believe that this ICC case or Palestinian efforts within the United Nations will bring about the creation of a Palestinian state. But don't listen to me; let me quote Dennis Ross, who has with admirable tenacity served presidents of both parties as a Middle East peace negotiator:

> "Since 2000, there have been three serious negotiations that culminated in offers to resolve the Israeli-Palestinian conflict...
> "In each case, a proposal on all the core issues was made to Palestinian leaders and the answer was either "no" or no response...
> "Palestinian political culture is rooted in a narrative of injustice[...] Compromise is portrayed as betrayal, and negotiations -- which are by definition about mutual concessions -- will inevitably force any Palestinian leader to challenge his people by making a politically costly decision...
> "But going to the United Nations does no such thing. It puts pressure on Israel and requires nothing of the Palestinians. Resolutions are typically about what Israel must do and what Palestinians should get. If saying yes is costly and doing nothing isn't, why should we expect the Palestinians to change course?"

In short, the ICC and the UN aren't about solving problems, they're about an unwillingness to negotiate and compromise for a true and lasting peace.

Finally, there is the question of the ICC and the United Nations itself. One anecdote, recently recounted by the Israeli ambassador, should suffice on the credibility of the United Nations writ large. Recently, the Conference of High Contracting Parties at the Fourth Geneva Convention convened for only the third time in their history to pass judgment on a country in violation of these important standards. Three times in history. Each time – this is almost incredible – has been to condemn the State of Israel. Not Syria. Not Iran. Not Burma or Cambodia or Sudan. Israel.

But going to the ICC is qualitatively different than going to the UN or invoking the Geneva conventions. At the UN the Palestinians and their supporters can get all the nonbonding resolutions they want at the General Assembly, but at the Security Council (which is the only

UN organ that could give meaningful, legally-binding support in their struggle with Israel, acting under Chapter VII of the Charter), they have always been stymied by the US veto. The ICC resembles the Security Council in its ability to provide meaningful support, but by design neither the US nor any other nation has the ability to block ICC action.

What Palestinian leaders want from the ICC ultimately is international criminal indictments, not just of individual members of the IDF and Israeli intelligence services, but most importantly, the national leadership of Israel—both its democratically elected leaders and its top military commanders and other officials of its security ministries. They want the Court to indict such officials and turn them into international fugitives, unable to leave Israel for fear of arrest. Their aim is to both harass them as individuals, and to delegitimize Israel by establishing as a fact that many of its top leaders have been indicted for war crimes and are being harbored by the Israeli government from international justice. So this has to be regarded as a serious escalation by the Palestinians.

Knowing that the US cannot veto ICC indictments, they are seeking them as an illicit form of pressure against their ostensible negotiating partner. And the ICC has already obliged them by opening a preliminary inquiry. Will the ICC go further and actually indict Israelis? It is too early to tell. Hopefully the ICC prosecutor and others who care about the ICC will resist the temptation to delegitimize the institution by ensnaring it in the political minefield of the Arab-Israeli struggle. But you can rest assured that a solid group of countries—the same ones that have forced three meetings under the Fourth Geneva Convention—intend to bring as much pressure to bear as possible on the Court to indict Israeli leaders. Whether the Court is able to resist such pressure—and whether it wants to—will be the greatest test it has faced in the 13 years since it came into existence.

The fact that Palestinian leaders are also now subject to ICC indictment is not a double-edged sword. Look no further than the ICC-indicted leader of Sudan, Omar Bashir, who is welcomed at Arab League summits and does not fear to travel in the Arab world. This demonstrates that, within their region, Palestinian leaders have nothing to fear from ICC indictments. But Israel's region is the West, and within the West such indictments are taken seriously and will be enforced to the degree possible. Fundamentally this is just another example of the Palestinians taking advantage of Western ideals and institutions, not to advance them, but to weaken and delegitimize them within their region.

All of this was foreseeable at the time that the ICC came into being. In fact, the US Congress foresaw it. That's why, in writing the American Servicemembers' Protection Act (ASPA), which aimed fundamentally to protect American military personnel and America's leaders from politically-motivated ICC investigations, Congress sought to provide similar protections to our Allies, and most importantly, to Israel. ASPA's authorization to use force to free persons detained by the ICC reads as follows:

SEC. 2008. AUTHORITY TO FREE MEMBERS OF THE ARMED FORCES OF THE UNITED STATES AND CERTAIN OTHER PERSONS DETAINED OR IMPRISONED BY OR ON BEHALF

OF THE INTERNATIONAL CRIMINAL COURT.
(a) AUTHORITY.—The President is authorized to use all means necessary and appropriate to bring about the release of any person described in subsection (b) who is being detained or imprisoned by, on behalf of, or at the request of the International Criminal Court.
(b) PERSONS AUTHORIZED TO BE FREED.—The authority of subsection (a) shall extend to the following persons:
(1) Covered United States persons.
(2) Covered allied persons.
(3) Individuals detained or imprisoned for official actions taken while the individual was a covered United States person or a covered allied person, and in the case of a covered allied person, upon the request of such government.
The term "covered allied person" was expressly defined in section 2013 of ASPA to include Israel, due to Congress's recognition of the risks that are now materializing:
(3) COVERED ALLIED PERSONS.—The term "covered allied persons" means military personnel, elected or appointed officials, and other persons employed by or working on behalf of the government of a NATO member country, a major non- NATO ally (including Australia, Egypt, Israel, Japan, Jordan, Argentina, the Republic of Korea, and New Zealand), or Taiwan, for so long as that government is not a party to the International Criminal Court and wishes its officials and other persons working on its behalf to be exempted from the jurisdiction of the International Criminal Court.

Mme. Chairman, members of the committee, over the last few decades, many provisions have been written into to law to leverage assistance to the Palestinian people in such a way as to incentivize peace and penalize terror. Since the Oslo Accords, about $5 billion in U.S. assistance has been transferred to the Palestinians. What has it bought? Peace? Certainly not. Territorial agreement? Far from it. The abandonment of terrorism or the commitment to the destruction of the State of Israel? Not really. A better life for the Palestinian people? Absolutely not.

The time has come to stand by both the letter and the spirit of the law. We cannot stop the Palestinian Authority or the Palestinian people from being their own worst enemies; we cannot stop them from posturing on the global stage or manipulating the United Nations to no good end; we can, however, stop subsidizing these feckless and dangerous quests and we can and must ensure that the ICC does not become a political tool aimed at the harassment of our allies, and ultimately, you can be certain, ourselves.

Thank you.

Ms. ROS-LEHTINEN. Mr. Makovsky.

STATEMENT OF MR. DAVID MAKOVSKY, ZIEGLER DISTINGUISHED FELLOW, THE WASHINGTON INSTITUTE FOR NEAR EAST POLICY

Mr. MAKOVSKY. Thank you very much, Madam Chairwoman Ros-Lehtinen, Ranking Member Deutch, members of the committee. Thank you for inviting me here today.

First, it is worth focusing on what is at stake for the Palestinians and for the ICC itself. Clearly, the Palestinian move for membership at the ICC is deepening the chasm between Israelis and Palestinians. The move is part of a Palestinian two-prong international strategy: Involve the U.N. Security Council; and go to the ICC.

For now, they have given up on direct talks with Israel. Of course, this is wrong. Direct talks are the only way to solve the problem and to promote peace. For the ICC, they also seem to be veering off course. For its part, the original ICC purpose has been to deal with mass atrocities and not serve as another politicized U.N. agency. If the ICC wants to be taken seriously, it should remain true to its origins and avoid politicization.

So what has just happened? When PA leader Mahmud Abbas signed the Rome Statute, he allowed for authority retroactive to June 13, just hours after three Israeli youths were kidnapped and subsequently murdered in the West Bank, to permit an investigation into last summer's Gaza war. ICC Prosecutor Fatou Bensouda announced a few weeks later that she would launch a preliminary examination without first determining if the PA is eligible to raise such a claim. Only Bensouda could determine if and when the preliminary examination ends, and transitions to a full-fledged investigation.

While the ICC previously inserted itself in the Congo war, there there were over 5 million deaths. In Gaza, the death toll was approximately 2,000 Palestinians, half of which Israel believes to be terrorists, and 65 Israeli soldiers.

The effect of this Palestinian approach is further deterioration in the relationship between Prime Minister Benjamin Netanyahu and President Abbas. In protest of the PA strategy, Israel is withholding $127 million each month in Palestinian tax revenue, which is unlikely to be released until a new Israeli Government is formed, perhaps in late May. The Israeli move, it should point out, given that it is a monthly move, is financially more consequential than anything the United States is undertaking.

Historically, the ICC investigations could take years. And so far, only two Congolese warlords have been convicted.

Israel's situation, needless to say, is dramatically different. It is a democracy. The ICC has no jurisdiction where there is a functioning judiciary. Following the Gaza war, Israel is in the process of indicting four Israeli soldiers for potential abuses. And the IDF has invited all NGOs—all—to come forward with evidence. In short, Israel's democratic judicial process negates the need for the ICC to step in. The consequences against Israel are not just going to be felt down the road. The mere investigation of Israel by the ICC is designed to put Israel under a cloud and to give a boost to the boycott, divest, and sanction—BDS—movement. Throughout the Gaza war Israel——

Ms. ROS-LEHTINEN. If the gentleman would suspend, the Chair notes that there is a disturbance of committee proceedings. The committee will stand in recess until the Capitol Police can remove these individuals.

[Recess.]

Ms. ROS-LEHTINEN. Thank you, Mr. Makovsky. Give us 1 minute to close the doors, and then you can begin your testimony. Thank you. You may begin, sir.

Mr. MAKOVSKY. Throughout the Gaza war, Israel and the PA continued their security cooperation in the West Bank. There is impressive professionalism in the Palestinian Security Services, thanks in part to training by the U.S. Security Coordinator and the high-level cooperation with their Israel counterparts. Media reports have suggested that Israel was able to divert troops from the West Bank to Gaza this summer because it knew that PA security services would maintain order. This is the bigger picture today.

Both have an interest in the not allowing the West Bank to return to chaos or to Hamas. Most Israelis do not want security cooperation to collapse. Israel would have to spend a lot of money and manpower that they do not have to make up for the loss of security cooperation, and this is especially dangerous at a time that they must be vigilant on other fronts against Hezbollah in the north and Hamas in Gaza. A lack of security cooperation would be devastating to the PA as well.

Abbas said this summer, "We don't want to go back to the chaos and destruction, as we did we did in the second intifada. We will not go back to an uprising that will destroy us."

This does not mean there shouldn't be punitive measures. The key is to ask if the penalty produces the result you want or if it is counterproductive. Withholding funding will lead to the collapse of the security cooperation and ultimately the PA, creating a vacuum that could be filled by radicalism, especially Hamas.

There should be a focus, I would argue also, on the ICC itself. The ICC has the authority to decide whether to move forward and go from a preliminary examination to a full investigation.

What can be done? First, the ICC should make it clear that it will not insert itself when the parties are engaged in conflict resolution. It will put this issue aside.

Second, the U.S. should proclaim clearly that we do not accept the PA move and urge the ICC to terminate its inquiry and encourage all of our allies to do the same, as Canada did.

Third, the Congress should bolster the Armed Services Protection Act of to 2002, which makes clear that our servicemen and allies, including Israel, will be protected from a politicized body.

In conclusion, the Palestinians should recognize the signing of the Rome Statute is unhelpful to their interests. As long as there is hope of conflict resolution, the ICC should avoid inserting itself. The international community should do everything it can to bring Israelis and Palestinians together to solve their differences and not deepen the divide between these two peoples. I look forward to the discussion.

Ms. ROS-LEHTINEN. Thank you very much.

[The prepared statement of Mr. Makovsky follows:]

Testimony before the House Subcommittee on the Middle East and North Africa
The Palestinian Authority's International Criminal Court Gambit:
A True Partner for Peace?

David Makovsky
Ziegler Distinguished Fellow and Director, Project on the Middle East Peace Process
The Washington Institute for Near East Policy

February 4, 2015

Chairman Ros-Lehtinen, Ranking Member Deutch, and Members of the Committee, thank you for inviting me to discuss the Palestinian Authority's move to the International Criminal Court (ICC). It is an honor to appear before you today.

Before I briefly review the chronology of the events and then suggest some ideas on where we go from here, I think it is worth focusing on what's at stake, not just for the Palestinians, but for the ICC itself.

I want to be clear from the outset that I see the Palestinian move for membership in the ICC as deepening the chasm between Israelis and Palestinians, and unfairly criminalizing the relationship between the two sides. Instead of bringing the parties closer together, the move creates a whole new arena of confrontation that could play out over years. We want the parties to solve their problems, and not to lock into a villain and victim narrative that would make conflict resolution impossible. This is bad not just for the Palestinians, but also for the ICC itself.

The purpose of the ICC is to deal with mass atrocities, and not serve as another politicized UN agency. It is hard to see how countries like the United States, whose membership the ICC actively seeks, will be attracted by such an overreach in applying the court's jurisdiction. The ICC Prosecutor Fatou Bensouda herself wrote in the *Guardian* op-ed, "It is my firm belief that recourse to justice should never be compromised by political expediency. The failure to uphold this sacrosanct requirement will not only pervert the cause of justice and weaken public confidence in it, but also exacerbate the immense suffering of the victims of mass atrocities. This, we will never allow." If the ICC wants to be taken seriously, and not be viewed like the Geneva-based UN Human Right Council that views Israel as an obsession at a time that 200,000 Syrians are being slaughtered, it should remain true to its origins and avoid politicization by inserting itself into a complex conflict such as the Israeli-Palestinian issue.

Here is the background to the Palestinian case. Just over a month ago, on December 30 -- the fiftieth anniversary of the founding of Fatah, the central component of the Palestine Liberation Organization -- Palestinian Authority (PA) leader Mahmoud Abbas signed twenty different international conventions, including the Rome Statute of the ICC. The name of the statute refers to the 1998 conference that established the treaty-based court, which began operations in 2002.

The main significance of the Abbas move is that it enabled the ICC to assert jurisdiction over future developments in the West Bank and Gaza Strip, and it empowers any signatory to the Rome Statute -- currently including 160 countries -- to claim that Israel should be brought to the court on charges of war crimes. Meanwhile, within approximately a week of Abbas' signing the Rome Statute, UN Secretary General Ban-Ki Moon publicly confirmed that the Palestinians will become an ICC member on April 1, 2015.

By January 16, ICC chief prosecutor, Gambian lawyer Bensouda, announced that she would start a preliminary examination into last summer's Gaza war. As such, Bensouda rejected an option at her disposal to first determine whether the PA is eligible to bring such a claim. Bensouda's decision does not come out of the blue. This past summer she penned an op-ed in the *Guardian* at the end of the Gaza war. On August 29, 2015, she wrote: "In November 2012, Palestine's status was upgraded by the UN general assembly to 'non-member observer state' through the adoption of resolution 67/19. My office examined the legal implications of this development and concluded that while this change did not retroactively validate the previously invalid 2009 declaration, Palestine could now join the Rome statute." We don't know if the Bensouda preliminary inquiry will transition to a preliminary examination in weeks, months, or years. Nobody knows but her. We should note the ICC has engaged in preliminary examinations against the United States in 2007 due to its role in Afghanistan. As far can be determined, the examination was never completed. There are also other preliminary investigations against both Britain and Russia that were not completed.

When Palestinians signed the Rome Statute, they attached a letter asking for an investigation into the Gaza war during last summer even though it predated their signing of the Rome Statute. It is curious that Abbas's letter calls for the investigation to occur on June 13, which not coincidentally is just hours after three Israeli youths were kidnapped and ultimately murdered at a hitchhiking post in the West Bank. Israel launched a manhunt for the boys the following day. The actual war began on July 8, when 210 rockets were indiscriminately fired by Hamas on Israeli cities. It is only thanks to the U.S.-funded Iron Dome anti-missile defense system that the Hamas rockets did not lead to scores of deaths. While the ICC previously inserted itself in the Congo war where just in a few years there were over five million deaths, in Gaza, we are talking about a death toll of 2,000 Palestinians -- approximately half of which are believed to be terrorists -- and sixty-five Israeli soldiers, as well.

Israeli officials are enraged by the move to the ICC. There is no counter-move so far to bring Hamas for an ICC investigation.

The net effect of this Palestinian approach is to lead to a further deterioration in the relationship between Prime Minister Binyamin Netanyahu and President Abbas. It is hard to negotiate with someone when you want the world to equate him with Serbia's Milosovec. There are indications that the number of Likud ministers in the Israeli government who want the PA to collapse has gone up, but so far, it does not include the Prime Minister or the professionals who deal with this issue. Yet, if the relations were terrible between the Israel and the PA before, it just got much worse.

It seems that the Palestinians move to ICC membership is part of a broader strategy. With Abbas turning eighty this spring, he has settled on a two-prong international strategy -- a move to the United Nations Security Council and bringing charges against Israel to the ICC -- and has given up on the idea of direct talks with Israel. It is unclear if he genuinely thinks the new strategy will be successful or rather he believes it is at least an appropriate legacy as he heads into the twilight of his political career. One Israeli security official said that 2015 is the year of the "international intifada," alluding to the Arabic term used for uprising against Israel.

In addition to the ICC, PA officials seem to believe salvation will come from the United Nations Security Council. They believe that shortly after the formation of a new Israeli government, the French will renew their draft to impose "terms of reference" in a United Nations Security Council Resolution (UNSCR) for ending the conflict between Israel and the Palestinians. This would involve a return to 1967 lines with some territorial exchanges or swaps and two capitals in Jerusalem. The Palestinians are hoping the Obama administration will either vote for it or abstain, but not wield a veto, which it has only done once in its six years in office. While there are routine UN General Assembly resolutions on the issue, it would be the first time that there would be a Security Council resolution to serve as a template to gain Palestinian statehood. Netanyahu has called the approach an imposed solution that Israel will reject. Yet questions remain whether the Palestinians could even accept an UNSCR that is to its overall liking, but includes some elements that they may not like. Can it accept the idea of a Jewish state? Limitations on relocation of Palestinian refugees? The Palestinians rescinded their support in December of a first draft of a proposed UNSCR that had even the smallest concessions.

In protest of the Palestinians' turn to internationalize the conflict both at the ICC and the UNSC, Israel is currently withholding approximately $127 million per month of Palestinian tax revenues, which has been key to Palestinians paying monthly salaries. PA Foreign Minister Riyadh Malki announced last week that the Palestinians are taking out loans to pay sixty percent of salaries for the month of January. Seventy-five U.S. Senators have now called on Secretary of State John Kerry to withhold American aid, as well. One should assume it is unlikely that the tax revenue will be released until a new Israeli government is formed, perhaps sometime in late May. Stopgap moves are required – such as assistance from Europe and the Arabs – until a new government is formed.

As noted above, the Israeli anger against the PA is genuine. It is hard to call someone a peace partner, if you believe he is openly calling upon you to be tried at the Hague. Conversely, the ICC investigation can take years and only two people have ever been convicted, both of which are Congolese warlords active in the brutal second Congo civil war, where 5.4 million people died from 1998 to 2007.

Israel's situation is dramatically different. Israel is a democracy. According to the complementarity clause of the ICC, the Court has no jurisdiction where there is a functioning judiciary to hold people accountable for their actions. Through the Tibon Committee set up after the Gaza war, Israel's Judge Advocate General (JAG) is in process of indicting four Israeli soldiers for potential abuses in 2014. The IDF has publicly invited NGO's and others to come forward to the JAG if it believes it has evidence. In short, the ICC only need step in where there is no democratic judicial process, and this is not the case in Israel.

Israel went to "extraordinary lengths" to prevent civilian casualties during this summer's conflict in the Gaza Strip, according to the Chairman of Joint Chiefs of Staff Gen. Martin Dempsey upon return from a visit to Israel after the Gaza War. Gen. Dempsey is in a better position to judge than myself as he sent a team out to look into this issue. "I actually do think that Israel went to extraordinary lengths to limit collateral damage and civilian casualties," said Dempsey during a forum at the Carnegie Council for Ethics in International Affairs in New York City. "In this kind of conflict, where you are held to a standard that your enemy is not held to, you're going to be criticized for civilian casualties," he added, according to Reuters.

The Hamas tunnels "caused the IDF some significant challenges," Dempsey said. "But they did some extraordinary things to try to limit civilian casualties, to include... making it known that they were going to destroy a particular structure." Dempsey listed Israel Defense Forces measures such as the "roof-knocking" and the dropping of warning leaflets as part of their attempts to protect civilian lives. "The IDF is not interested in creating civilian casualties. They're interested in stopping the shooting of rockets and missiles out of the Gaza Strip and into Israel," Dempsey argued.

The American general recounted that an American delegation visited Israel three months ago to learn lessons from the conflict, "to include the measures they took to prevent civilian casualties and what they did with tunneling."

During the fifty days of fighting, Hamas fired thousands of rockets and mortars at Israeli towns and cities, including Tel Aviv, and used a sophisticated tunnel network to carry out attacks on Israeli military encampments in southern Israel, close to the Gaza border. Some of the tunnels also had exits abutting Israeli civilian communities, giving Hamas the ability to attack them as well.

Israel's ratio of civilian to military casualties in Operation Protective Edge was only one-fourth of the average in warfare around the world, a former commander of British forces in Afghanistan Col. (res.) Richard Kemp told the Knesset Foreign Affairs and Defense Committee in September.

"No army in the world acts with as much discretion and great care as the IDF in order to minimize damage. The US and the UK are careful, but not as much as Israel," he told the committee.

Israel seems to be unfairly maligned with the ICC investigation. Moreover, it is being singled out as there is no ICC investigation to a real bloodbath, the killing in Syria, for example. The UN Security Council has not even referred the Syria issue to the ICC.

Yet, the consequences against Israel are not just going to be felt down the road. The mere investigation of Israel by the ICC is designed to put Israel not just on the defensive, but also to put Israel under a cloud and give a boost to the BDS -- boycott, divestment and sanctions -- movement. This effort to delegitimize Israel is an existential threat -- not less than the Iranian nuclear issue.

However, Israel is correct to do its own internal inquiry and ensure that all is done to prevent innocent Gazans from being hit despite the fact that Hamas is deliberately putting their lives in jeopardy. Israeli leaders say Israel uses rockets to protect civilians while Hamas uses civilians to protect their rockets.

The PA is wrong to take their case to the ICC. While anger at the PA for making the move is justified, the question remains whether one is inviting bigger risks if the PA concludes that non-payment of salaries could lead it to disband. Abbas has threatened it many times, but so far the PA has remained intact. How long can the PA go without paying salaries without imploding? If the PA does implode, who will fill the vacuum? It seems the force that will gain the most for the PA disbanding will be Hamas. In short, greater radicalism can ensue in the event of a vacuum. Therefore, one must not seek penalties that are counter-productive.

It is worth noting that as bad as things were during the Gaza war this past summer, Israel and the PA continued their security cooperation in the West Bank. Both do not want to see Hamas return to the West Bank or to allow public unrest to reach a critical mass. There is a level of professionalism in the Palestinian security forces -- thanks in no small measure due to the training of the U.S. Security Coordinator over the last decade -- and cooperation with their Israeli security counterparts that was unthinkable in the 1990's when the security services were completely politicized. There have been media reports that Israel was allowed to divert troops from the West Bank to Gaza because it knew that the PA security services maintained cooperation.

I would argue that this is still the bigger picture today, since both have an interest that the West Bank does not return to chaos of the past. While there is little likelihood for tax revenues to be transferred until after the Israeli elections and a new coalition is formed later this spring (which will require stopgap aid from the Arab states and Europeans), most Israelis and most Israeli security professionals do not want security cooperation to collapse. This is not in Israel's interest. They would have to spend billions of shekels and a lot of manpower that they do not have to make up for the loss of security cooperation. At a time that the Israeli military must be vigilant against Hezbollah attacks in the north and Hamas attacks from the south, Israel would prefer not to have to divert manpower to the West Bank. It should be added that without this security cooperation, a return of chaos to West Bank cities would be devastating for the Palestinian Authority, as well. Indeed, at a speech in June in Jedda, Saudi Arabia in front of the Organization of Islamic Cooperation, Abbas publicly defended security cooperation in very emphatic terms. "We don't want to go back to chaos and destruction, as we did in the second (Palestinian) intifada (uprising)," he said. He continued, "I say it openly and frankly. We will not go back to an uprising that will destroy us."

In short, both sides depend on this security coordination. We cannot forget the bigger picture. Yet, this does not mean that there should be no punitive measure taken against the PA for its move to the ICC. The key thing is to ask if the penalty produces a result that you want or whether it is counterproductive. Withholding funding -- over time -- will lead to the collapse of the security cooperation and ultimately the PA, creating a vacuum that can be filled by radicalism. I remember arguing against a cut-off of funds before this distinguished panel in 2011. I said at the time that sadly the people who will be hurt the most by the cut-off will be then Palestinian Prime Minister Salam Fayyad. Indeed, Fayyad was scapegoated by other factions in the PA for the loss of money and he was forced out of office. So, we should be very careful in wielding the cut-off of funds. Most of American assistance pays Palestinian debts to Israeli energy companies. About a quarter of the aid is humanitarian, unrelated to the PA. Even security aid to Palestinians goes to adequate training for security cooperation. It does not go to pay Palestinian salaries.

So what can be done? First, I think the ICC should make clear that it will not insert itself when the parties are engaged in conflict resolution. Secretary of State Kerry certainly has illustrated the depth of his commitment to resolve this conflict. Second, I think we should proclaim clearly and loudly that we do not accept the PA membership move at the ICC and encourage our allies to declare the same, while urging the ICC not to conduct its inquiry. Canada has told the ICC that it does not recognize Palestinian statehood and so we will not be bound by its judgments and we will urge our allies to take a similar approach. More broadly, we should say an ICC that engages in such action will be viewed in an unfriendly manner by the United States. This is not how a relatively new international institution should act at a time that it wants its jurisdiction to be respected by the international community. Third, I would hope the U.S. Congress would bolster the Armed Service Protection Act of 2002, which makes clear our views that our own servicemen including our allies -- of which Israel is listed -- will be protected from the reach of a potentially politicized body.

I would hope the Palestinians would recognize that signing the Rome Statute is unhelpful to their interests, and I hope the ICC realizes that its actions cannot occur in a vacuum. As long as there is a hope of conflict resolution, the ICC should avoid inserting itself. We should not forget that the international community must do everything in its power to bring Israelis and Palestinians together in order to solve their differences and not be a prod to deepen the chasm between the two peoples.

Ms. ROS-LEHTINEN. Excellent testimony.

And I thank our Capitol Police for helping us to restore order so that we can hear our panelists calmly.

I will begin with you, Professor. You have outlined several issues of jurisdiction and other legal problems with the ICC that should have precluded the ICC from accepting this non-existent state of Palestine to its membership. As we all know, the prosecutor has already launched a preliminary examination. Could you briefly—briefly—walk us through the steps that must be taken from start to finish for an investigation to take place? Does an investigation have to be initiated by the Palestinians against Israel? Can it be initiated by anyone on behalf of the Palestinians? And also the Palestinians attached a letter asking for an investigation into last summer's Gaza conflict when they signed the Rome Statute. Is it a reasonable reading of the legislation to say that when the Palestinians submitted this letter, they initiated the investigation because the preliminary examination is the start of the process and that cutting off the PA's funds would be consistent with the intent of the legislation? Also the administration's diplomatic efforts have clearly not been effective in preventing Abu Mazen's actions at the U.N. and at the ICC. So I ask our panelists, is there a better way that we can be leveraging our assistance, perhaps not to the Palestinians themselves, but to the international allies of the Palestinians or at the U.N.? Professor, we will begin with you about what kicks in the——

Mr. KONTOROVICH. So the Palestinians submitted instruments of accession to the Rome Statute, joining the Rome Statute, which is purely prospective. They also submitted with that a 12(3) declaration. A 12(3) declaration is a mechanism to give the court retroactive jurisdiction going back over particular incidents, and they did this back to the Gaza war, after the three boys were kidnapped and killed.

When a country joins the ICC, any country can demand, can refer a situation to the prosecutor. It doesn't have to be one of the countries involved. Any other member country can do so. Now only the prosecutor actually does the investigations, but the process of kicking that off begins with, for example, countries referring such a situation.

In the case of the 12(3) declaration, the 12(3) declaration does not require any subsequent follow up or referral by countries. So it does seem that, within the meaning of the existing legislation, the 12(3) declaration, which has resulted in the initial preliminary examination, is the thing that initiated the process.

Now, the current legislation, existing legislation, speaks of the Palestinians initiating a judicially authorized investigation. So there is two parts of that to parse, initiating and judicially authorized. Now clearly the steps they have taken can count as initiating. Obviously, the Palestinians themselves don't work at the ICC, so they can't be the ones to actually sign off on the investigation, and if it actually means opening an investigation at the ICC, it would be reading the legislation to be meaningless if it would require the Palestinians doing that, since they can't do that because they are not part of the ICC.

The question of a judicially authorized investigation is a separate question because after the prosecutor completes her preliminary examination, which involves questions like jurisdiction, just a very basic question—is there anything to think about here—she can then go to the Pre-Trial Chamber, a body of the ICC, and ask them for authorization to open an investigation. The statute could be read to say that is what actually triggers the aid cutoff because that is what a judicially authorized investigation is. But it has already been initiated. It is consistent with the intent of the legislation to say that the first step of this process is what is going to initiate it, and that step has, indeed, been taken.

However, there are other steps that can be taken about funding under existing legislation, if I may briefly add. Existing statutes provide no funds authorized to be appropriated under this or any act shall be available for the United Nations or any specialized agency which accords the PLO the same standing as member states. Now it is important to point out that this statute, unlike other ones, does not speak of membership. It doesn't say if the U.N. gives membership to the PLO or to the Palestinians, rather if it gives them standing otherwise enjoyed by member states.

Ms. ROS-LEHTINEN. I am going to just cut you off there a second just because I am—I know you didn't finish your thought, but what about leveraging our assistance. What is the panelists' view of how we should do that, if we should change or not?

Mr. SCHANZER. Madam Chairman, I would say that there are a few areas that I think are worth visiting in terms of the funds that we provide the PA. One is we should, as much as the foreign ministry within the PA pursues these activities at the ICC and at the U.N., we should make sure that whatever allocations are cut off immediately. The same I would say would go for the Presidential office. There is a slush fund that Mahmud Abbas uses to pursue these aims, and I think we could earmark those funds and cut them. Any area of the PA that is influenced by the PLO decision-making also we should cut off. I mean, basically, what we are talking about is conditioning our aid, which is something that we have not done. We basically need to demand good governance on the part of the Palestinian Authority.

The Palestinian Authority itself, though, I should note, is not the problem. They are basically a bureaucratic functionary government that is making sure that sewage and electricity and water flows. We are really concerned here with the decisionmaking of cronies of Mahmud Abbas within the PLO and the Fatah faction. They should be the target of any subsequent investigation.

Ms. ROS-LEHTINEN. Thank you so much.

And just 1 minute, Ms. Pletka and Mr. Makovsky.

Ms. PLETKA. There is no question we need to be careful not to cut off our nose to spite our faces in terms of aid to the Palestinians, and there are important parts of that assistance that go to the Palestinian people and that don't go to security assistance that again would cause more problems. I want to highlight something I left out from my testimony very fast.

Ms. ROS-LEHTINEN. If you could make it quick because we messed up on the clock so I am probably out of time, but 30 seconds.

Ms. PLETKA. I am going to read you half a sentence from what AID reported to CRS as what a lot of the aid is used for: It goes to the PA toward paying off its commercial debt. Direct budget support will be used in the same manner as previous transfers to service debt to commercial suppliers and commercial banks.

Do you realize that aid to the Palestinians is going to pay off their commercial debts, that they are making all those choices on their own? That can't happen.

Ms. ROS-LEHTINEN. Point taken. Thank you so much.

Mr. Deutch is recognized.

Mr. DEUTCH. Thank you, Madam Chairman.

I just want to follow up, Mr. Makovsky, with Ms. Pletka's last comment about aid and what might happen and just ask you directly. Walk us through what would happen if the PA were to run out of money, if they were unable to pay salaries or were to collapse. What impact would that have on the Palestinians? What impact would that have on Israel?

Mr. MAKOVSKY. Thank you, Congressman. It is a good question. I think if they don't pay salaries, then we are going to see a cutoff in the security cooperation. I think it is a matter of time. There could be a stopgap move between now and the end of May. Maybe the Europeans and the Arabs would do more until then, but this is a major move. Israel would, I think, have to pay billions of shekels, a lot of money in terms of manpower to step in in terms of order, in terms of all to assume its civilian responsibilities. It is not something Israel relishes to do, and I can tell you just returning now from Israel and talking to the professionals involved in this issue, this is not something they want. So I think it is a big deal.

Just also to respond to Madam Chairwoman's point about the aid and where it goes and what Danny said, yes, right now a lot of the money basically goes to the Israeli electric company to pay debts that has been incurred in Gaza and the West Bank for heating. Basically, in the last few years, of the $440 million, $70 million goes to security assistance. The next tranche is in November. That is still a while. The 370 is broken into two parts, $170 million for USAID project assistance, and 200 in direct budgetary assistance to the PA. But, frankly, given a lot of problems in the last 2 years, my understanding is a lot of that does not go to the PA. It doesn't go to salaries. And, frankly, it has gone to more humanitarian projects. So that is the flexibility of the Congress of that 370 to kind of fashion it the way it wants. But Danielle is right, that a lot of the money right now basically goes to the Israel companies where there is heating bills that are owed in the West Bank and Gaza.

Mr. DEUTCH. I want to just go back to the bigger picture of the decision to go to the ICC, which strikes me as really just a diversion. It is a diversion from problems within the PA, and the bigger issue is the fact that there is this effort to go to the ICC at the same moment when the PA is still trying to sort out what role Hamas is to play with them.

Now, we have had hearings on that in the past. I would love someone on the panel to speak to where things stand from your perspective with respect to the relationship between the PA and Hamas, the role that Hamas continues to play, the reports that

Hamas has essentially thrown up its hands and said that its up to the PA now to decide what to do with Gaza. Where are those relations, and how is it that we are ultimately able to go forward at all until we sort out the fact that there is no place for a terrorist group within the Palestinian Government?

Mr. MAKOVSKY. Could I take a very quick brief, and then yield to my colleagues, because just returning, this has been a big issue for me on my trip when I was over there. What is clear is you have a standoff between the PA and Hamas. Basically, the idea of the summer was to get the PA back into Gaza, but the PA doesn't want to go into Gaza because Hamas still has guns in Gaza. As one Palestinian said to me, David, they have got three roles for us, three jobs for us, Hamas. They want us to be their doormen to let them in and out of Gaza. They want us to be their ATM machine. And they want us to be their building contractors. But everything else is them, and they have got the guns.

You have got Sisi of Egypt, the President of Egypt, who wants the PA drastically to come back into—because he just called the Izz ad-Din al-Qassam a terrorist organization, the first time that I am aware of that any Arab country has called the Hamas militant wing a terrorist organization. I think it is a welcome development. But the point is you have a standoff. The Egyptians want the PA to do more, and the PA doesn't want to go in there because it thinks that it is a booby trap situation in Gaza, and they will never really be able to assert control. So they want to wide Hamas out.

In the meantime, nothing is moving. One apparently senior Hamas person said to someone, Hey, if there is a siege going on, I have to admit we can't blame the Israelis. It is the PA that doesn't want to come in. But from their perspective, it is a security threat, and so, in the meantime, we just have a standoff.

Mr. DEUTCH. You say they want to wait it out.

Dr. Schanzer, what does that mean for U.S. policy? They want to wait it out, and yet there is still an existing relationship that we have take into account, don't we?

Mr. SCHANZER. Well, we absolutely do. The way this is structured is Hamas is trying to get the PA to make the Gaza strip more Halal, if you will, for international donors. You put sort of the face of the PA on a Hamas-controlled territory. That would allow for the flow of goods and services. The PA has not given up on this. Abbas truly would like to bring Gaza back under his control. This is still an aim of his, and as long as this continues, it is going to create a very problematic dynamic, both in terms of ICC in terms of recognition here, aid, and I don't think it has been addressed properly yet.

Mr. DEUTCH. Thank you. I yield back.

Mr. DESANTIS. Thank you, Madam Chairman.

The Hamas-Fatah, you have seen terror attacks, suicide attacks, rocket attacks, human shields, so they want to go to the ICC. Obviously, they are in a situation where they would be liable, and yet, Ms. Pletka, you said that it is not really going to be much of a double-edged sword. Can you elaborate on, you know, why would some Arabs want to go to these western institutions and think that that could give them an advantage, given that we could easily identify examples in which they would be liable?

Ms. PLETKA. Well, I think this goes actually to the question that Mr. Deutch asked as well, which is, you know, why go to the ICC right now? It is just a distraction. And I think for a lot of the countries that seek to internationalize their claims, not just the Palestinians, but others, it is an option for them where they can have their cake and eat it too. They are not subject to the penalties that come along with these because they are not actually part of a system of rule of law. And if you don't have rule of law, then of course, the jurisdiction of the ICC or of any other international organization is completely irrelevant.

Now, we haven't signed onto it, but this really is something that, you know, this is the reason that the American Service-Members' Protection Act was written. It is because these self-executing international organizations that are not subject to the veto of any particular country are increasingly popular with groups like the Palestinians but also others—the Cubans, the Venezuelans, the Irans, sadly, the Russians, and others who seek to use them. And frankly, most of them don't give a damn about the Palestinians. They care about going after us. That is why it is much more of a distraction.

As for Hamas, they don't care. Look, they just found a new headquarters. We were just talking about this. Where is their headquarters? It is in a NATO-allied country. Is that okay? Apparently. Apparently, yes, it is okay. You know, if it doesn't matter to them and it doesn't matter to us, guess what, it doesn't matter to anybody.

Mr. DeSANTIS. And so I know the ICC is separate from the U.N., but if you look over the years at how the U.N. has ganged up on Israel, we could see that the ICC would likely be in a similar—they would probably have a similar perspective?

Ms. PLETKA. I think for the ICC the question has always been whether the member parties, the party stays to the Rome Statute and the actual staff of the International Criminal Court care more about the institution or care more about their political axes to grind, and this is the moment of truth for them. If they go forward with this, with this completely contradictory, as you have all noted, this notion that an occupied territory that is also a state, that also has standing, that it can also bring a case against another country that isn't a party—we could go on with the contradictions here— if they decide that they want to go forward with this, then I think it is the beginning of the end of the ICC as a viable institution. That is a choice for them.

Mr. DeSANTIS. Yes, sir.

Mr. KONTOROVICH. Yeah, I want to add to that.

Mr. DeSANTIS. Your mike. Just put your mike on.

Mr. KONTOROVICH. So it seems at first a mystery why the Palestinians, who use rocket attacks on civilian cities as a primary strategy in war, why they would wish to avail themselves of the ICC. And some people who are optimists say, well, this is a wonderful salutary development because it shows the Palestinians want to open themselves up to accountability and international justice.

But it is important to understand what the ICC can do and has done. Its track record shows that it is incapable of rendering impartial justice in an ongoing, bilateral conflict. It is not some well-established Olympian seat of judgment; rather, it is a weak, conflicted, and floundering institution beset by all sorts of problems.

The last two times they tried to go after an incumbent regime that did not want to be prosecuted—and this was just in the past few months—the prosecution of the President of Kenya and the President of Sudan, both of those cases collapsed due to the noncooperation of those countries. And in particular, in the Kenyatta case, the cooperation was subtle and there have been no sanctions against Kenya for this. And, basically, the Kenya proceedings have proven to be a playbook—and many international commentators have said this—for countries who wish to not cooperate with ICC jurisdiction.

Now, in the Kenya case, what they did was intimidate witnesses. Now, in Gaza, the witnesses are pre-intimidated, right. In a place where you shoot 20 collaborators in a day, nobody is going to go and point out to ICC investigators where the Hamas rocket launches were. So they can really win both ways. They have the appearance of accepting international responsibility while in practice, de facto, having impunity.

Mr. DeSantis. And this idea that—some would say it is a good sign they want to be held accountable. I know Secretary Kerry has pledged money. I know countries like Qatar have pledged a lot of money to "rebuild the Gaza strip." And I think a lot of people like me see the kind of rinse and repeat where Hamas will use that money to rebuild tunnels, acquire more rockets.

So is anyone on the panel, can you weigh in on, are we just repeating ourselves with that money going down there? Is there any evidence that that money is actually being used to rebuild it in a different way, or are we going to just see more tunnels and more rockets?

Mr. Schanzer. Well, actually, the good news right now is that the international community is very gun shy about actually delivering these funds. Look, there is a downside of that, of course, which is the Palestinian people are suffering as a result of not enough aid coming in, but there is a sense now that it is not rinse and repeat, that the international community has gotten wise to the process that you have described. And so I think now there is going to be cause for greater accountability in the way that money flows to the Gaza strip.

Mr. DeSantis. I am out of time, and I will yield back.

Ms. Ros-Lehtinen. Thank you so much.

Mr. Cicilline of Rhode Island.

Mr. Cicilline. Thank you, Madam Chair.

Thank you very much for your testimony. The U.S., as you all noted, is not a party to the Rome Statute and obviously doesn't provide financial support to the ICC. Are there any levers that are available to the United States that would allow us to assert some pressure on the court not to pursue a case? And second part of that question is, is there any likelihood that there might be an allied country who would pursue actions against the Palestinian authority if their action subjects them now to jurisdiction of the ICC to sort of take advantage of that event?

Mr. Kontorovich. Let me address the existing mechanisms. Indeed, there are mechanisms to pressure the ICC. Now, much of the

direct pressure is limited because already we have so little cooperation, but it is important to identify the real bad guy here. According to the ICC prosecutor, she is not the one who decided unilaterally that the Palestinians are a state. Rather, she says it is the
United Nations who decided that the Palestinians are a state. And
in her statement, she said she is completely bound by the decision
of the General Assembly.

Now, under existing law, any agency of the United Nations
which gives the Palestinians the same standing as a member state
must have its funding cut off immediately. Now, standing is something short of membership. So it doesn't mean membership; it
means things other than membership. If it turns out that the vote
of the General Assembly gives the Palestinians the opportunity to
automatically join the ICC without any inquiry, substantive inquiry into whether they actually are a state, that is something only
reserved otherwise so far for U.N. member states.

That means, quite astonishingly, and it is a big thing, that the
U.N. itself or the General Assembly could face an aid cutoff. Now,
of course, that is not something one should do immediately. Rather,
one should seek clarification from the General Assembly: Did they,
in fact, in this vote intend to create automatic ICC standing for the
Palestinians with, of course, the explanation and the full disclosure
that if their answer is yes, that would trigger consequences under
U.S. law?

It is likely that the representatives of the United Nations would
respond, No, we did not have any such intention. We were simply
voting an internal symbolic thing, internal to the General Assembly
that has no consequence—which is true, and that is actually correct—that has no consequences beyond the General Assembly. And
that is right, but it is important to get them on record as saying
that, firstly, because if the ICC prosecutor is right then we have
to cut funding to the United Nations. If the ICC prosecutor is
wrong, then she has to dismiss the investigation involving Israel.

Mr. MAKOVSKY. Can I just, what I said in my remarks, I think
we should follow what the Canadian Government is doing. The Canadian Government has said we don't recognize Palestine as a
state—which is true, by the way, not just for the U.S. but also for
Europe—for almost all of Europe—and, therefore, we don't agree
with the premise of their membership, and therefore, we are not
going to cooperate with any ICC investigation in this regard. I
think that would be powerful. And the fact that the Canadians
have already taken that first step, I think, is something that we
should emulate and urge our allies to do the same.

Ms. PLETKA. But, Mike, I mean, we already don't cooperate with
the ICC in any meaningful way. We don't provide them with any
assistance. So, you know, those are nice words, but I don't think
that they are going to be a death blow to the investigation.

Mr. MAKOVSKY. Well, I mean, we are talking about, our allies are
members of the ICC, and so, therefore, it is meaningful.

Mr. CICILLINE. Thank you.

My final question is, is it the position of the panel that the filing
of charges by the ICC is the event that under existing U.S. law requires funding to be terminated, or is it the association with the

ICC? In other words, what is the event under current U.S. law that requires funding to the PA to be, you know, ended?

Mr. KONTOROVICH. It is definitely well short of charges. Charges are at the conclusion of a judicial investigation. So the statute is, unfortunately, a bit ambiguous. It could be the opening of an investigation, which is the next step but before the step of charges, or it could be the current step of a 12(3) referral, which automatically launches a preliminary inquiry.

Now, the language is ambiguous. It is consistent, I think, with the clear intent of the legislation for the funding to be—for the trigger to be the 12(3) declaration, which triggers the preliminary investigation. And so it is really a matter of legislative intent and interpreting ambiguous terms.

Mr. CICILLINE. Thank you.

I yield back.

Ms. ROS-LEHTINEN. Thank you so much.

Dr. Yoho.

Mr. YOHO. Thank you, Madam Chair.

I appreciate the panel being here. Last March, right here in this same committee room, we had a meeting on terrorism, nonproliferation, and trade on the subcommittee where we had testimony from Edwin Black saying that the money that we give to the Palestinian authority, it is fungible, and it indirectly supports PLO payments going to Palestinians, and/or their families, who have been accused or convicted of terrorism.

And last Congress, after that meeting, I introduced legislation that called on the PA to halt payments until that practice is stopped and Resolution 21 and 23 in their laws remove that. Since then, it seems like they have changed how that money is going, and it is going directly from the PLO to the terrorist.

What suggestions do you have in stopping this practice totally? Because we are giving that money to the Palestinian authority into the Middle East, which has received probably, per capita, more money than anyplace else in the name of peace, but yet we are not getting that. And so how do we stop that? If we truly want peace, are we just going to play the cat-and-mouse game and the shell game of moving stuff around?

So I would like to hear from you, Dr. Schanzer, start with you and down the line.

Mr. SCHANZER. Sure. Thank you, Congressman Yoho.

The answer to your question is, I am not exactly sure that that dynamic has shifted to the PLO just yet. There was an indication when the unity government was formed last spring that they were going to shift it to the PLO and would basically exonerate the PA——

Mr. YOHO. Right.

Mr. SCHANZER [continuing]. Out of the crosshairs of Congress. It is my understanding that even though they plan to do that, they have not shifted those responsibilities, and I couldn't tell you exactly why that has happened.

Mr. YOHO. Okay. To me, that is unacceptable. And where I come from, people don't want any money going there, especially if we are getting it in the name of peace and we are not accomplishing that. I mean, we are all adults here; we need to stop playing games if this is truly what we want. And I want to hear from you guys. We will go down real quick. I am down to 3 minutes.

I am not going to try to pronounce your last name.

Mr. KONTOROVICH. It is actually phonetic. Kontorovich.

So I just want to briefly shift the emphasis of the inquiry from the money we are giving to the Palestinians, which is a very complicated lever. As you have heard from lots of people on the committee, there is lots of tensions. If you take away the money, maybe the Palestinian authority will collapse. Israel has mixed feelings. I think it is useful to think of other ways of pressuring the Palestinians without messing with their money.

And I would point out briefly, money to Israel could be used in a way which would strongly check the current Palestinian——

Mr. YOHO. I need to correct you, that money is our taxpayers' money that we are giving in good faith. So if we are going to do that, I want the results for that or I don't want to support giving that money to them.

Ms. Pletka, can I hear from you?

Ms. PLETKA. I think the law is pretty clear. And I think the legislative intent is also pretty clear. I think the time has come to put a stop to it. You know, I think that the simplest thing is something I have said to this committee many, many times before, which is that all aid should be visited on a very periodic and frequent basis.

Mr. YOHO. I agree.

Ms. PLETKA. Stop it, look at it, and decide year to year exactly how it meets your needs. And this provides an opportunity to have that sort of strategic——

Mr. YOHO. Let me hear from Mr. Makovsky.

Mr. MAKOVSKY. It is an excellent question. I don't think the answer is good enough for the question, frankly. There are some things that, believe me, I have spoken to them, that the U.S. Congress scares the daylights of them.

Mr. YOHO. Good.

Mr. MAKOVSKY. For example, there was the whole issue last summer of Qatar moving salaries to people in Gaza, and the PA said we can't touch this or the United States Congress is going to shut us down. So sometimes Congress has more of a deterrent club than it realizes, and I hope it makes its point forcefully on the issue of aid to the terrorist families too because I think it is an important point.

Mr. YOHO. I appreciate it.

And then let me ask you this: Which aid program or policy would you suggest we here in Congress scale back or reform? And, again, this raises the question of we already have laws preventing ICC from being funded. Would it be more prudent for the U.S. to concentrate on reforming funding to the U.N. agencies which seem to be supporting the Palestinian until we get clarification on what they are doing? Dr. Kontorovich.

Mr. KONTOROVICH. Again, under current law, might actually give Congress and the United States an extraordinary, surprisingly broad leverage to cut off funding from the United Nations in general. And, obviously, that is a serious action, but in the shadow of that action and the availability of that sanction under existing law gives the United States a lot of power and leverage to demand concrete reforms.

If, for example, the General Assembly has gone beyond its role under the United Nations charter and is creating countries, that counts very powerfully for seriously revisiting funding to the United Nations as a whole.

Mr. YOHO. And I appreciate that. And that is a serious action, but these are serious times, and I think it is time we take serious action. Thank you for your time.

I yield back.

Ms. ROS-LEHTINEN. Thank you so much.

And we are going to try to get Mr. Boyle's questions in. We have a series of votes. Thank you.

Mr. BOYLE. Thank you, Madam Chair.

I was wondering, given that we are about 6 weeks away from Israeli election on March 17 and especially given the constant jockeying that is happening between Hamas and the Palestinian authority, I was wondering to what extent you believe the next 6 weeks will be a destabilizing time for the Palestinian community and Palestinian leadership, particularly given that the latest polls in Israeli election show it literally within possibly one seat?

Mr. MAKOVSKY. Look, I would say, what I said in my remarks, I think they need to find stop gaps because it is not just the election of March 17. There probably won't be a government until the end of May because it takes a long time; there is a lot of jockeying formation. And, therefore, you know, this is not something that is going to be solved tomorrow. I don't think in an election mode Israel is going to change its policies. So I think the PA has to look elsewhere.

If you want to talk about ideas about the Israeli election, I am happy to discuss in a different format, but I don't want to muddy the waters here on that.

Mr. BOYLE. Did anyone else have a comment on that?

Mr. SCHANZER. Look, I would just add this, by "destabilizing," if you mean that the Palestinians would be willing to perhaps restart a conflict or challenge the Israelis in other ways, I think that right now the PA is probably realizing that anything that they do—and Hamas is probably realizing the same thing—would probably help Netanyahu, and this is the guy that they hope to see lose during the election. So I think the conventional wisdom is that all of the actors might try to keep quiet during this time.

I think the ICC bid has been, to a certain extent, to gift to Netanyahu, quite frankly, saying, look, these are the people that we are trying to negotiate peace with and look what they are doing. And so I would expect over the next several weeks for there to be relative calm.

Mr. BOYLE. Well, that is certainly logical—and we would expect that—although, in one sense, one could say that the leadership or the behavior of Palestinian leadership has, in many ways, dictated Israeli elections all the way for the last 20 years.

The other question I had was, especially given what happened in Lebanon just in the last week, the latest on the relationship between Hezbollah and the Hamas. I know that is a little bit more broad than specifically the ICC issue, but of course all these are interconnected.

Mr. MAKOVSKY. If I could, by the way, just add to what John said, I just want to be clear that, I was in Ramallah a couple weeks ago, and what is different this time than the previous election cycle, as it seems to me, is the PA is far more passive than they usually are. They are usually inviting Israeli political delegations, giving interviews on Israeli television. Abbas did that regularly in the last two cycles. This time he isn't. Sometimes—I think this time he is thinking differently. He said on the Security Council and he said in his Arab League speech 2 weeks ago in Arabic that there is going to be no change no matter who wins.

That is why I think he wants this to be the year of the international intifada. Go ICC with one hand; U.N. Security Council on the other hand. And I, personally, think it will boomerang on him, but I think that seems to me his approach, which is he is in a kind of post-Israel phase, from his perspective. I think it is a terrible mistake.

On the Hamas-Hezbollah, I don't see the connection right now. I mean, they seem to be very much in different spheres. And Hezbollah is also, you know, intervening in the Syrian Civil War. There was a back and forth we saw the last couple weeks, but the Israelis I talked to on the security side did not expect a major escalation with Hezbollah because they think Hezbollah's intentions are elsewhere. So you know, we shall see.

And I should say, in terms of the Israeli elections, often security arrangements, security incidents traditionally have helped the more rightwing elements in Israel in elections. But if there was attacks from Gaza, it could go the other way since you have a government that was in charge and said we took care of this problem. Anyway, we will have to see. Let's all hope for a peaceful time toward the elections and certainly beyond it for both of these people.

Ms. ROS-LEHTINEN. Thank you so much, sir.

And I apologize to Ms. Ming and Mr. Higgins, but we have a series of votes, including debate time. Is there anything that you would like to make a statement about before we adjourn the subcommittee?

I will submit it for the record. Thank you, Mr. Higgins. Without objection.

Ms. Meng, my apologies to you. I will be glad to come back. Okay. I just don't know. It will be a long time.

Witnesses, thank you so very much for being with us, and audience members and Capitol Police.

And with that, the subcommittee is adjourned.

[Whereupon, at 3:29 p.m., the subcommittee was adjourned.]

APPENDIX

MATERIAL SUBMITTED FOR THE RECORD

SUBCOMMITTEE HEARING NOTICE
COMMITTEE ON FOREIGN AFFAIRS
U.S. HOUSE OF REPRESENTATIVES
WASHINGTON, DC 20515-6128

Subcommittee on the Middle East and North Africa
Ileana Ros-Lehtinen (R-FL), Chairman

January 29, 2015

TO: MEMBERS OF THE COMMITTEE ON FOREIGN AFFAIRS

You are respectfully requested to attend an OPEN hearing of the Committee on Foreign Affairs, to be held by the Subcommittee on the Middle East and North Africa in Room 2172 of the Rayburn House Office Building (and available live on the Committee website at http://www.ForeignAffairs.house.gov):

DATE: Wednesday, February 4, 2015

TIME: 2:00 p.m.

SUBJECT: The Palestinian Authority's International Criminal Court Gambit: A True Partner
                 for Peace?

WITNESSES: Jonathan Schanzer, Ph.D.
                 Vice President for Research
                 Foundation for Defense of Democracies

                 Mr. Eugene Kontorovich
                 Professor of Law
                 Northwestern University School of Law

                 Ms. Danielle Pletka
                 Senior Vice President
                 Foreign and Defense Policy Studies
                 American Enterprise Institute

                 Mr. David Makovsky
                 Ziegler Distinguished Fellow
                 The Washington Institute for Near East Policy

By Direction of the Chairman

COMMITTEE ON FOREIGN AFFAIRS

MINUTES OF SUBCOMMITTEE ON _____ *Middle East and North Africa* _____ HEARING

Day__*Wednesday*__Date_____*2/4/15*_____Room_____*2172*_____

Starting Time ____*2:05PM*____Ending Time ____*3:29*____

Recesses |__*0*__| (____to____) (____to____) (____to____) (____to____) (____to____) (____to____)

Presiding Member(s)

Chairman Ros-Lehtinen

Check all of the following that apply:

Open Session ☑   Electronically Recorded (taped) ☑
Executive (closed) Session ☑   Stenographic Record ☑
Televised ☑

TITLE OF HEARING:

The Palestinian Authority's International Criminal Court Gambit: A True Partner For Peace?

SUBCOMMITTEE MEMBERS PRESENT:

Chairman Ros-Lehtinen, Ranking Member Deutch, Reps Wilson, Weber, DeSantis, Yoho, Clawson, Zeldin, Connolly, Cicilline, Meng, Frankel, Boyle.

NON-SUBCOMMITTEE MEMBERS PRESENT: *(Mark with an * if they are not members of full committee.)*

N/A

HEARING WITNESSES: Same as meeting notice attached? Yes ☑ No ☐
(If "no", please list below and include title, agency, department, or organization.)

STATEMENTS FOR THE RECORD: *(List any statements submitted for the record.)*

SFR - Rep. Connolly

TIME SCHEDULED TO RECONVENE _____
or
TIME ADJOURNED ____*3:29*____

Subcommittee Staff Director

Statement for the Record
Submitted by Mr. Connolly of Virginia

Negotiations for a long-lasting peace must not be circumvented. The Palestinian Authority's application to join the International Criminal Court (ICC) is a counterproductive provocation that undermines the peace process. The devastation and humanitarian crises that define the Israeli-Palestinian conflict should expedite a return to the negotiating table, not inspire incendiary acts that undermine peace talks and perpetuate a cycle of violence. It is crucial that we not abandon the only framework that currently offers a roadmap to peace in the region.

The United States must be seen as an honest, independent broker able to bring both sides to the table. We must keep in mind that a negotiated peace is in the interest of all parties - Israelis, Palestinians, and their neighbors. Secretary Kerry is to be commended for his commitment to the peace process. Those who criticize Secretary Kerry's attempts at reviving negotiations should consider the alternative. It is a region embroiled in conflict and misery and a fate we should not accept for the Middle East.

The Palestinian Authority (PA) has made several attempts to bypass the peace process through unilateral declarations, and Congress has repeatedly rebuffed this approach. House Resolution 268, which passed in the 112th Congress by a vote of 407-16, urged Palestinian leaders to cease these efforts immediately. Unfortunately, the PA disregarded Congressional guidance and pursued a UN Security Council Resolution in December of last year that would have dictated a deadline for establishing a Palestinian state. This cynical maneuver, which failed to garner enough votes for approval, further imperiled hopes for cooperation and dialogue.

The Administration recently submitted a proposed budget to Congress for FY2016. In the FY2016 Budget for the Department of State, Foreign Operations, and Related Programs, the Administration has requested $440 million in funding for the West Bank and Gaza. The funding request includes $370 million in Economic Support Fund (ESF) assistance administered by the U.S. Agency for International Development (USAID) through grants to contracting organizations and direct budgetary assistance to the PA. The PA would also receive $70 million in International Narcotics Control and Law Enforcement (INCLE) funding for PA Security Forces (PASF).

These funding request levels are constant from FY2015. However, for the previous year's appropriations, Congress placed a restriction on the ESF component of assistance to the West Bank and Gaza that is relevant to today's discussion. For FY2015, ESF funds cannot be used for USAID projects in the West Bank and Gaza or for the direct support of the PA if "the

Palestinians initiate an International Criminal Court judicially authorized investigation, or actively support such an investigation, that subjects Israeli nationals to an investigation for alleged crimes against Palestinians."

Funding for the PA has traditionally received diverse support due to its impact on security and governance in the region. Cooperation between the Israeli Defense Forces (IDF) and the PASF has been integral to West Bank security and the vacuum created by a weakened or collapsed PA would likely be filled with a much less acceptable alternative.

The State Department has correctly condemned the PA's bid to join the ICC and is currently conducting a review to determine if ESF funds must be withheld pursuant to prohibitions placed on FY2015 appropriations. This review is a mechanism devised and authorized by Congress, and we should await its findings. In the meantime, we cannot allow the PA's diversion to drive us further from a negotiated peace. This is not in the best interest of the region or the security of Israel, a close and longstanding ally of the United States.

www.ingramcontent.com/pod-product-compliance
Lightning Source LLC
Chambersburg PA
CBHW080520290526
45790CB00006B/2244